ASIAN FAIRY TALES

Books LLC®, Wiki Series, Memphis, USA, 2011. ISBN: 9781157228592. www.booksllc.net
Copyright: http://creativecommons.org/licenses/by-sa/3.0/deed.en

Table of Contents

Asian fairy tales
How the Daughter-in-Law Got the Coins 1
Saat Bhai Champa 2
Thakurmar Jhuli 2
The Bronze Ring 3
What the Rose did to the Cypress 4

Chinese fairy tales
Beauty and Pock Face 5
The Pot Bears a Son 5
The Pretty Little Calf 6
The Water Mother 6
The Wolf of Zhongshan 6
Ye Xian 7

Indian fairy tales
Diamond Cut Diamond 8
Jackal or Tiger? 8
The Fisher-Girl and the Crab 9
The Jogi's Punishment 9
The King Who Would Be Stronger Than Fate 10
The Snake Prince 10
The Tiger, the Brahmin and the Jackal 11

Indonesian fairy tales
Bawang Putih Bawang Merah 11
Damarwulan 13
Panji (prince) 14

Japanese fairy tales
Bunbuku Chagama 16
Hanasaka Jiisan 17
Issun-bōshi 17
Kachi-kachi Yama 18
Momotarō 18
My Lord Bag of Rice 20
Schippeitaro 20
Shita-kiri Suzume 21
The Boy Who Drew Cats 21
The Cat's Elopement 22
The Crab and the Monkey 22
The Fountain of Youth (fairy tale) 23
The Husband of the Rat's Daughter .. 23
The Stonecutter 24
The Tale of the Bamboo Cutter 24
Urashima Tarō 26

Korean fairy tales
Janghwa Hongryeon jeon 27
The Fox Sister 28

Malaysian fairy tales
Preeta Samarasan 28

Turkish fairy tales
Madschun 29
The Boy Who Found Fear At Last 29
The Silent Princess 30

Vietnamese fairy tales
The Hundred-knot Bamboo Tree 30
The Story of Tam and Cam 31

Introduction

Purchase of this book entitles you to a free trial membership in the publisher's book club at www.booksllc.net. (Time limited offer.) Simply enter the barcode number from the back cover onto the membership form. The book club entitles you to select from hundreds of thousands of books at no additional charge. You can also download a digital copy of this and related books to read on the go. Simply enter the title or subject onto the search form to find them.

Each chapter in this book ends with a URL to a hyperlinked online version. Type the URL exactly as it appears. If you change the URL's capitalization it won't work. Use the online version to access related pages, websites, footnotes, tables, color photos, updates. Click the version history tab to see the chapter's contributors. Click the edit link to suggest changes.

A large and diverse editor base collaboratively wrote the book, not a single author. After a long process of discussion and debate, the chapters gradually took on a neutral point of view reached through consensus. Additional editors expanded and contributed to chapters striving to achieve balance and comprehensive coverage. This reduced the regional or cultural bias found in many other books and provided access and breadth on subject matter otherwise little documented.

How the Daughter-in-Law Got the Coins

How the Daughter-in-Law Got the Coins is a Sri Lankan fairy tale collected by H. Parker in *Village Folk-Tales of Ceylon*.

It is Aarne-Thompson type 982, Ungrateful Heirs.

Synopsis

A man marries a rich woman who did not help his mother. He gives his mother a bag full of pottery shards. The mother contracts leprosy, but since she shakes the bags where the daughter-in-law can hear and announces that whoever cares for it will have, the daughter-in-law tends her. After the mother dies, the woman realizes it was shards, not coins.

Variants
The tale is widespread, with many ways to trick the heirs into thinking there is wealth to be had.

Source (edited): "http://en.wikipedia.org/wiki/How_the_Daughter-in-Law_Got_the_Coins"

Saat Bhai Champa

Saat Bhai Champa or **Sat Bhai Chompa** is a popular folk tale in the Bengal region of South Asia. The story was first officially published by Dakshinaranjan Mitra Majumder in the book Thakurmar Jhuli in 1907. The introduction to Thakurmar Jhuli was written by Nobel-Laureate, Rabindranath Tagore. More detailed version of the story was published by Bishnu Dey under the name "Sat Bhai Champa" in 1944. Several Bengali movies were made based on the Saat Bhai Champa story. Sat Bhai Chompa (1968) movie is ranked by British Film Institute as one of the top ten Banladesh film of all time.

Plot
Once upon a time, there lived a king. The king was not able to produce any heir to the throne through his three wives. The king was depressed and spent large amount of time by himself in the forest. A priest in the forest saw the king's misery and gave him fruits of bearing. The priest instructed the king to feed the fruits to his wives and then they would conceive children. The king gave his three wives the fruits as instructed by the priest. Two elder queens did not produce any children. However, the younger queen gave birth to octuplets: seven boys and one girl. The elder queens became jealous and buried the babies in the garden before the younger queen gained consciousness from pregnancy. The babies magically blossom into seven champak flowers and a trumpet flower. The last baby, the girl, was born some time after first seven babies in a time when the elder queens left the room with seven babies and this enabled the maid to hide the baby from the elder queens and named the child Champa. Elder queens, then, placed seven puppies on the younger queen's bedside and claimed the queen gave birth to seven puppies. Champa grew up in the forest. After learning her origin from her maid, she helped to revive her brothers into princes.

Another variant of the story has it that seven babies turned into seven puppies.

Sat Bhai Chompa 1968 Movie
The movie was made in East Pakistan, what is now Bangladesh. The director of the movie is Dilip Shom and main casts are Kabori and Khan Ataur Rehman. The movie is ranked by British Film Institute as one of the top ten Banladeshi film of all time.

Saat Bhai Champa 1978 movie
The movie was made in West Bengal, India. The movie was directed by Chitrasarathi and music of the film was composed by Raghunath Das. The actors starring are Biswajeet, Sandhya Roy, Mrinal Mukherjee, Gita Karmakar, Biswanath Chattopadhyay and Chhanda Chattopadhyay

Saat Bhai Champa 1994 movie
This movie was made in Bangladesh. The movie is a remake of 1968 movie.

Arts
Saat Bhai Champa painting by Gaganendranath Tagore is considered a masterpiece in contemporary Indian painting. The painting is currently located at Academy of Fine Arts of Calcutta.

Source (edited): "http://en.wikipedia.org/wiki/Saat_Bhai_Champa"

Thakurmar Jhuli

Thakurmar Jhuli (*Grandmother's Tales*) (Bengali: ঠাকুরমার ঝুলি) is a collection of Bengali folk tales and fairy tales. Dakshinaranjan Mitra Majumder was the person who first collected some folk-stories of Bengal and published it under the name of *Thakurmar Jhuli* in 1907 (1314 of Bengali calendar). The Nobel-Laureate, Rabindra Nath Thakur wrote the introduction to the compilation. Since then, it has become a favourite of Bengali children. Over the years, it has become a household name in West Bengal and Bangladesh.

Some characters and stories like Lalkamal-Nilkamal and Byangoma-Byangomi have gained a legendary status, especially among the children. Hundreds of edition of the book have been published from Bangladesh and West Bengal since the original publication. An English translation by Rina Pritish Nandy has been available lately.

Some other comparable books for children in Bengali Literature by the same author are *Thakur Dadar Jhuli* (Grandpa's Sack of Folktales), "Dadamoshayer Tholay" (Maternal-Grandpa's Sack of Folktales) and "Thandidir Tholay" (Maternal-Grandpa's Sack of Folktales)

Content of Thakurmar Jhuli
- The Introductory Song

Book 1: *Dudher Sagar (The Ocean of Milk)*
- *Kalabati Rajkanya (The Elusive Princess)*
- *Ghuomonto Puri (The Sleepy Mansion)*
- *Sat Bhai Champa (Flower brothers and their sister)*
- *Kankanmala Kanchanmala (The curse of the needles)*

- *Sit Basanta (The Two brothers)*
- *Kiranmala (The Strange Children of The King)*

Book 2: *Roop Tarashi (Scary Beauty)*
- *Nilkamal And Lalkamal (The magnificent adventures of the two princes)*
- *Dalimkumar (Controlled by the seed)*
- *Patal Kanya Manimala (The Girl from the deep)*
- *Sonar Kathi Rupar Kathi (The gold-stick and the silver-stick)*

Book 3: *Chang Bang (The Nest of the Animals)*
- *Sial Pundit (The Cunning Fox)*
- *Sukhu and Dukhu* (Friend Of The Animals)
- *Bramhan Bramhani* (The clever wife of the foolish bramhin)
- *Der Angule* (One and a half inched)

Book 4: *Aam Sandesh (The Dessert)*
- *Sona Ghumalo (It's Bedtime)*
- *Sesh (The End)*
- *Furalo*

Source (edited): "http://en.wikipedia.org/wiki/Thakurmar_Jhuli"

The Bronze Ring

The Bronze Ring is the first story in *The Blue Fairy Book* by Andrew Lang. According to Lang's preface, this version of this fairy tale from the Middle East or Central Asia was translated and adapted from *Traditions Populaires de l'Asie Mineure* by Carnoy et Nicolaides. (Paris:Maison-neuve, 1889.)

Unlike the great majority of the stories that follow it in Lang's work, this fairy tale is not well-known.

Synopsis

The king despairs because his castle is surrounded by wasteland, instead of a fruitful garden. Advised that the remedy is a head gardener "whose forefathers were also gardeners", he finds such a man. Under this gardener's care the land does flourish, but a new problem arises.

The princess loves the gardener's son – and will marry no one else. After she refuses her father's choice of a husband (the prime minister's son), he contrives a contest to settle the matter: the two men must go to a far destination and the first to return shall marry the princess. They do not go off on an equal footing. The Minister's son is equipped with a fine horse and gold, while the gardener's son is given a lame horse and copper.

Traveling swiftly, the minister's son encounters a woman in rags. Weak and starving, she begs for his help. He spurns her.

The gardener's son then encounters the woman. Generously, he gives her his purse and invites her to ride behind him. At the next city, heralds announce that the sultan is sick, and that whoever cures him can name the reward. The woman instructs the boy: find and slay three particular dogs, burn them and collect their ashes, then make way to the sultan. Place the dying sultan in a cauldron over a roaring fire, and boil him right down to his bones. Finally, arrange the bones properly and scatter the dogs' ashes over them. The gardener's son does all these things and the sultan revives, in full hearty youth. Exactly as the witch suggested, the gardener's son chooses the bronze ring for his reward and will accept nothing else. This ring contains a djinni who grants any wish. Now the gardener's son continues his journey in a fabulous sailing ship, with a cargo of gems, sails of brocade and a hull of gold, crewed by a dozen handsome sailors, each dressed as richly as a king – all gifts of the bronze ring.

Eventually he meets his rival, who has spent all his fortune. Unrecognized, the gardener's son offers to supply his rival with a ship - on the condition that the skin of his back be branded with the imprint of the bronze ring, heated in a fire. Once that is done, the gardener's son asks the ring to prepare a ship with half-rotten timbers painted black, ragged sails and a maimed and sickly crew. In this ship the prime minister's son returns, and claims his bride from the king.

As the unhappy princess' wedding is being prepared, the king looks out on the harbor and wonders at the gleaming gold ship sailing into it. He is so taken by the sight of its captain (the gardener's son) that he invites him to the wedding and, after closer inspection, actually invites him to give away the bride.

The gardener's son agrees, but when he sees the intended groom he objects, telling the king that the man is not worthy of the princess, being nothing more than his own slave. The prime minister's son denies this, but the brand of the bronze ring on his back serves as proof of the claim. The gardener's son marries the delighted princess that day with the king's blessing. They have a short period of happiness.

Meanwhile, a student of the black arts has come to learn about the djinni of the bronze ring. When the prince sails off for a trip in his golden ship, he persuades the princess to trade him the ring for some red fish. Once he has the ring, he wishes the prince's boat from gold into rotten wood, his crew from princely appearing men into hideous slaves, and the cargo of gems into ravenous black cats. (In the first edition of 'The Blue Fairy Book', reflects racist European stereotypes of the times, the magician is a crafty Jew and the debased crew become Negroes.)

Realizing that an enemy must now have his bronze ring, the prince sails on until he comes to an island inhabited by mice. The Mouse Queen sends an envoy to ask that the ship sail away with its terrible cargo of cats. The prince agrees, on the condition that his bronze ring be found and returned to him. The Mouse Queen contacts all the mice of the world, three of whom know that the magician keeps the bronze ring in his pocket when awake, and in his mouth when asleep. The three go to retrieve the ring. One of them tickles the sleeping magician's nose with her tail, and he expels the ring from his mouth with a sneeze. After some misadventures, the mice manage to return the ring to the prince, who restores his golden vessel and hurries home to the princess. He captures the magician and has the man broken into pieces by being tied to the tail of a savage mule.

Source (edited): "http://en.wikipedia.org/wiki/The_Bronze_Ring"

What the Rose did to the Cypress

What the Rose did to the Cypress is a Persian fairy tale. Andrew Lang included it in *The Brown Fairy Book*, with the note "Translated from two Persian MSS. in the possession of the British Museum and the India Office, and adapted, with some reservations, by Annette S. Beveridge."

Synopsis

A king had three sons. The oldest went hunting and chased a deer, giving orders that it should be captured rather than killed. It led him to a sandy waste where his horse died. He found a tree with a spring beneath it and drank. A faqir asked him what he did there. He told him his story and asked the faqir's, repeating when the faqir put him off, until the faqir told him he had been a king, and his seven sons had all tried to win a princess whose hand could only be won by answering the riddle, "What did the rose do to the cypress?" and died for their failure. His grief sent him into the desert.

This inspired the son with a love for the same princess. His attendants found him and brought him back, but he grew ill for love, and his confidants found this out and revealed it to the king. The king made arrangements for him to go. At the city, the princess's father tried to dissuade him. He was asked, failed, and was executed. His second brother followed and likewise died.

Finally the third went, but having reached the city, he saw his brothers' head and went to a nearby village, where he took shelter with an ancient, childless couple. Disguising himself, he searched the city for the secret, and found he could get into the princess's garden by a stream. There he hid, but when the princess sent her maids for water, they saw his reflection and were terrified. The princess had her nurse bring him to her. He answered her questions at random, convincing her that he was mad, but his beauty made her protect him as her own. Dil-aram, who had seen him first, grew fond of him and begged him to tell her what he was about; finally, he was convinced she was in love with him, told her his story, and promised to marry her and keep her among his favorites. She could not answer the riddle, but knew that a certain negro from Waq of the Caucasus had told the princess it.

The prince set out to Waq of the Caucasus. An old man advised him on how to arrive there, despite the jinns, demons, and peris. He should take this road until it split, then take the middle road for a day and a night, where he would find a pillar. He should do what was written on the pillar. He found a warning where the roads split, against the middle road, but took it and came to a garden. He had to pass a giant negro to reach it, and a woman there tried to persuade him from his way. When she failed, she enchanted him into a deer.

As a deer, he came to lead a band of deer. He tried to jump from the enchanted garden but found that it would bring him back where he had jumped from. The ninth time, however, the other deer vanished. A beautiful woman there took him as a pet. He wept, and the woman realized he had been enchanted by her sister. She turned him back, gave him a bow and arrows, a sword, and a dagger, that had all belonged to heroes, and told him that he must seek out the home of the Simurgh, but she could not direct him to it.

He obeyed her directions about the Place of Gifts, where wild animals lived, and a lion-king gave him some hairs, saying he must burn them for aid. He disobeyed her directions to avoid the castle of clashing swords, because whatever was fated to happen to him would happen, and fought the negroes there. With the lion's aid, he defeated them, rescuing a princess, and gave it all into the lion's care until he was done with his quest.

He found the Simurgh's nest, where only the young ones were, and killed a dragon there; then he fed the hungry young birds on it, and they slept, being full. When their parents returned, the lack of noise convinced them that the prince had killed and eaten their young, but the mother bird insisted on checking to discover the truth, and the young ones woke. The Simurgh carried him to Waq, and gave him three feathers, any of which would summon him.

At Waq, he learned that only the king knew the riddle and went to court. He gave the king a diamond and said it was his last treasure. The king wished to please him, but the prince wanted only the answer to the riddle. When he asked, the king said he would have killed anyone else, but when the king went on asking what the prince wanted, the prince refused to ask for anything. Finally, the king told him that he could have what he wanted, if he consented to die afterward. He was the cypress, and his wife, whom he had brought before them in chains and rags, was the rose. He had once rescued peris and restored their sight, and in return, they had arranged for his marriage to a peri princess. She had betrayed him, riding off every night to a negro who beat her. The king had killed him and his fellows, except the one who escaped to tell the princess with the riddle. He then told the prince to prepare for execution. The prince asked only for a final washing, but when washing, he summoned the Simurgh, and it carried him off.

He returned. On the way, he married the princess from the castle of clashing swords, and the woman who had disenchanted him. At the city, he demanded the negro whom the princess hid beneath her throne to confirm the truth of his words. He told the story, and the king having found the negro, he confirmed it. Instead of marrying the princess, he took her captive, had the head decently buried, and sent for Dil-aram.

At home, the prince had the negro torn apart between four horses. The princess begged for mercy; those who had died had been fated to die, and it was her fate to be his. He forgave her, married her and Dil-aram, and lived happily with his four wives.

Source (edited): "http://en.wikipedia.org/wiki/What_the_Rose_did_to_the_Cypress"

Beauty and Pock Face

Beauty and Pock Face is a Chinese fairy tale collected by Wolfram Eberhard in *Chinese Fairy Tales and Folk Tales*.

It is classified as *Cinderella*, Aarne-Thompson type 510A, the persecuted heroine; others of this type include *The Sharp Grey Sheep*; *The Golden Slipper*; *The Story of Tam and Cam*; *Rushen Coatie*; *The Wonderful Birch*; *Fair, Brown and Trembling* and *Katie Woodencloak*. Indeed, it is sometimes titled *Cinderella* in English translation.

Synopsis

The older of two sisters, the child of the first wife, was beautiful and called Beauty, but her younger sister, the child of the second wife, had a pocked face and was called Pock Face. The first wife had died when her child was young and come back as a yellow cow. The wicked stepmother abused Beauty and set her tasks. The yellow cow did them for her, but the stepmother found out and had the cow killed. Beauty collected the bones and put them in a pot. One day, her stepmother did not take her to the theater, so Beauty broke everything at home, including the pot; when she did that, a horse, a dress, and a pair of shoes come out. She put on the clothing and rode the horse, but she lost one shoe in the ditch. Men came by, she asked them to get her the shoe, and each one agreed if she would marry him. She refused a fishmonger for smelling of fish, a rich merchant for being covered with dust, and an oil merchant for being greasy, but agreed to marry a scholar.

Three days after the wedding, Beauty went to pay her respects to her parents. Pock Face lured her to the well, pushed her in, and sent word to the scholar that she had contracted small pox. After a time, she went herself and explained her looks by the illness. Beauty, however, had become a sparrow and came to taunt Pock Face while she was combing her hair; Pock Face taunted her back. The scholar heard and asked her to come to a cage if she were his wife; she came. Pock Face killed the sparrow and buried it. Bamboo shot up on the grave. The shoots tasted delicious to the scholar but gave Pock Face ulcers on her tongue. Pock Face cut the bamboo down and had a bed made from it, but though the scholar found it comfortable, it poked Pock Face with needles, so she threw it out. An old woman took it home. She found that dinner was cooked for her whenever she came home. In time, she caught Beauty, who had her give her some cooking things, which enabled her to appear.

Beauty gave the old woman a bag to sell by her husband's house. When she did so, the scholar questioned her and brought her back home. Pock Face proposed tests to determine who was the genuine wife. First they walked on eggs; Beauty did not break any, and Pock Face broke them all, but she would not admit it. Then they climbed a ladder of knives; Beauty did not cut her feet, and Pock Face did, but she would not admit it. Finally, they jumped into boiling oil; Beauty emerged alive, but Pock Face died. Beauty sent her body back to her stepmother, but her stepmother thought it was carp. When she saw it was her daughter, she fell down dead.

Motifs

The series of transformations can not only be found in the similar *The Story of Tin Tin From L/doon*, but in other fairy tales, such as *A String of Pearls Twined with Golden Flowers* and *The Boys with the Golden Stars*; *Sweetheart Roland* includes fewer transformations, but also has the heroine appearing secretly to do housework for a benefactor.

Source (edited): "http://en.wikipedia.org/wiki/Beauty_and_Pock_Face"

The Pot Bears a Son

The Pot Bears a Son is a Uighur fairy tale collected in *Folk Tales from China*.

It is Aarne-Thompson type 1592B, The Pot that Died.

Synopsis

Nasrdin Avanti borrowed a big pot from a rich and stingy man. Then he congratulated him: the pot had had a child. He gave him the small pot as well. Then he borrowed the pot again and returned to mournfully tell him that the big pot had died. When the rich man objected, he said that if it could bear a son, it could no doubt die as well.

Variants

A form of this tale also appeared in *The Book of the Thousand Nights and One Night*.

Source (edited): "http://en.wikipedia.org/wiki/The_Pot_Bears_a_Son"

The Pretty Little Calf

The Pretty Little Calf is a Chinese fairy tale collected by Wolfram Eberhard in *Folktales of China*.

Synopsis

An official without children left home to take up his post. His first wife said she would offer him gold on his return; the second, silver; the third, a son. He was pleased with the third wife, but the other wives were jealous. When she bore a beautiful son, they claimed she had borne a lump of flesh; the first wife threw the baby into a pond, but he floated, and so the second wife had him wrapped in straw and grass and fed to a water buffalo. When the official returned, his first wife gave him gold, the second silver, and when he heard that his third wife had borne a horrid lump of flesh, he sentenced her to grind rice in a mill.

The water buffalo gave birth to a beautiful calf with a hide like gold. It was very fond of its master, who always gave it some of his food. One day, the official said that if it understood human speech, it should bring the dumplings he gave it to its mother. The calf brought them not to the water buffalo but to the repudiated wife. The first two wives realized that it was the son. They claimed to be ill; the first wife said she needed to eat the calf's liver, and the second, that she needed the calf's skin. The official let the calf loose in the woods and bought another to kill.

A woman named Huang had announced she would throw a colored ball from her house, and whoever caught it would be her husband. The calf caught it on its horn. Miss Huang realized that she had to marry it. She hung the wedding robes on its horns, and it ran off. She chased it and found a young man in wedding robes by a pond; he told her to come, she said she had to find her calf, and he told her that he was the transformed calf. He went back to his father and told him the truth. The official was ready to kill his first two wives; his son persuaded him to pardon them, but he had his son bring back his mother from the mill.

Commentary

The calumniated wife is a common motif. Many European fairy tales feature the woman who claims that she will give a man a child, and the enemy who removes the child, but the enemies are usually the woman's sisters, who did not make such a claim and so are jealous, or her mother-in-law. Closely related to this tale are tales *The Boys with the Golden Stars*, and *A String of Pearls Twined with Golden Flowers*, in both of which the promised children are done to death, and return in other form, although, unlike this one, they return in a wide variety of forms because the enemy continually discovers their new forms and kills them; in *A String of Pearls Twined with Golden Flowers*, her enemy is more similar to this tale, as the villain is the husband's old favorite, whereas in *The Boys with the Golden Stars*, it is her mother-in-law. More commonly, European tales feature the children being abandoned: *The Dancing Water, the Singing Apple, and the Speaking Bird*, *The Tale of Tsar Saltan*, *The Three Little Birds*, *The Wicked Sisters*, *Ancilotto, King of Provino* and *Princess Belle-Etoile*.

Some of the stories motif has similarities with the stories from *One Thousand and One Nights*, namely Tale of the Trader and the Jinni. The marital transformation also figures in European tales, such as *Hans My Hedgehog*, *The Pig King*, and *The Donkey*.

Source (edited): "http://en.wikipedia.org/wiki/The_Pretty_Little_Calf"

The Water Mother

The Water Mother is a Chinese fairy tale collected by Wolfram Eberhard in *Folktales of China*. It does not exist in early text, although the cult of the Water Mother existed from the time of the Sung dynasty.

It is Aarne-Thompson type 565. Other tales of this type are *Sweet Porridge* and *Why the Sea Is Salt -- Why the Sea Is Salt* also using it as an explantory legend.

Synopsis

A woman lived with her mother-in-law and daughter; though she was dutiful, her mother-in-law hated her. One day, she decreed that they could not buy water from water-carriers, but her daughter-in-law would have to carry it from the well. The work was too hard for her, but she was beaten when she failed. One day, she thought of drowning herself in the well. An old woman told her not to, and gave her a stick to strike the pail with. She was to tell no one and to never strike twice.

For a time, she was happy, but her mother-in-law spied on her, stole the stick, and struck the pail twice. This caused a flood that drowned many houses and her daughter-in-law. The pail had become a spring. Afterward, a temple was raised for the daughter-in-law, and they called her the Water Mother.

Source (edited): "http://en.wikipedia.org/wiki/The_Water_Mother"

The Wolf of Zhongshan

The **Wolf of Zhongshan** (Chinese: 中山狼傳; pinyin: *Zhōngshān Láng Zhuàn*) is a popular Chinese fairy tale deals with the ingratitude of a creature after being saved. The first print of the story is found in the Ming Dynasty *Ocean Stories of Past and Present* (Chinese: 海說古今; pinyin: *Hǎishuō Gǔjīn*) published in 1544.

Synopsis

The story is set during the late Spring and Autumn Period. King Jian of Zhou was leading a hunting party through Zhongshan when he happen to come across a wolf. King Jian takes aim with his bow and arrow but misses and hits a stone instead. The wolf desperately flees through the forest with the hunting party in pursuit. As the wolf makes it way through the forest he stumbles upon a traveling Mohist scholar Mr. Dongguo (Chinese: 東郭先生; pinyin: *Dōngguō Xiānshēng*). The wolf appeals to the scholar's belief of "universal love" and implores for his help. Mr. Dongguo takes pity on the creature and hides it in one of his books bags strapped to his donkey.

When the hunters approach him, Mr .Dongguo denies any knowledge of the wolf's whereabouts. After the hunters had left Mr. Dongguo lets the wolf out of his bag, got on his donkey and was about to take his leave only to be stopped by the wolf. The wolf now asked the scholar to save his life again, this time from starvation. Mr. Dongguo offered the wolf some pastries, but the wolf smile and said "I don't eat those, I dine solely on meat". Puzzled, Mr. Dongguo inquires if the wolf intended to eat his donkey and the wolf replies "No, no, donkey meat is no good". The donkey, upon hearing this, bolts from the scene as fast as its four legs to carry it leaving Mr. Dongguo behind with the wolf. To Mr. Dongguo's surprise, the hungry wolf pounced on him and announced it intention to eat him. When Mr. Dongguo protests at the wolf's ingratitude, the wolf presents the argument: since the scholar saved his life once why not do it again? Now that it was starving, only by serving as the wolf's food will the scholar have fulfilled the act of saving his life. Besides, the wolf complained that it nearly suffocated while it was crammed in the scholar's bag and the scholar now owed him. Dongguo and the wolf debated and finally decided to present their case to the judgment of three elders.

The first elder they present their argument to is an old withering apricot tree. The tree relates its own experience to the two on how when it was young, children used to pick its fruits from its branches and the tree would tell them to eat their fill. Now it was about to be chopped down to provide firewood. The tree sides with the wolf. The wolf is very pleased.

The second elder they present their argument to was an elderly water buffalo. The buffalo tells its story of how it served its masters for many years dutifully providing him with milk and plowing his fields. Now his master wants to butcher it so he can eat his meat. The buffalo too sides with the wolf. The wolf grins and feels even more justified in his request to eat the scholar. Mr. Dongguo reminds the wolf that they have one more elder to seek out.

The last elder they present their argument to is an elderly farmer. The farmer was skeptical and didn't believe that the wolf could fit into the bag. To illustrate its point, the wolf crawled back into the bag and right away the old farmer tied up the bag and started to beat the wolf with his hoe. The farmer bashes the wolf to an inch of his life then unties the bag and drags his dying wolf out of the bag.

Seeing the pitiful wolf the scholar thinks that the old farmer was too cruel but just then a weeping woman comes running towards them. She pointed to the wolf and told Mr. Dongguo and the farmer how it dragged off her little boy. Mr Dongguo now no longer pitied the wolf. He picked up the hoe and strikes the final blow to the wolf's head.

Author

The authorship of this text is a matter of dispute. The text originally appeared in the *Hǎishuō Gǔjīn* as an anonymous text with no author listed but it has generally been attributed to Ma Zhongxi (Chinese: 馬中錫; pinyin: *Mǎ Zhōngxí*) (1446–1512). In classical Chinese literature, this tale is quite unusual in the fact that it is a fully developed animal fable. In most prose fables or poems where animals are imbued with human characteristics (Huli jing), they are usually first transformed into human form before they are allowed to speak.

The term Mr. Dongguo (*Dōngguō Xiānshēng*) has now become a Chinese idiom for a naive person who gets into trouble through being softhearted to evil people.

Variations

Another variation of this tale can be found in the *Precious Scroll of Shan Cai and Long Nü*.

Source (edited): "http://en.wikipedia.org/wiki/The_Wolf_of_Zhongshan"

Yeh-Shen: A Cinderella Story From China

Ye Xian (Simplified Chinese: 叶限; **Traditional Chinese**: 葉限; **pinyin**: Yè Xiàn) or in the southern part, **Yeh-Shen** is a Chinese fairy tale that resembles the European Cinderella story (but about a millennium older) and the Malay-Indonesian Bawang Putih Bawang Merah tale. It is one of the oldest known variants of *Cinderella*, first published in the 9th-century compilation *Miscellaneous Morsels from Youyang*.

Plot

A scholar named Wu, who is chieftain of a community of cave-dwellers, had two wives and a daughter by each of them. Yeh-Shen is Wu's beautiful daughter of one wife, and she is intelligent, artistic and gifted in many skills such as pottery and poetry. In contrast her half-sister, Jun-li, is spoiled, self-interested and lazy.

When her mother and then her father die from a local plague, Yeh-Shen is forced to become a lowly servant and work for her father's other wife, named Jin (Yeh's evil stepmother) and her daughter, Jun-li. Despite living a life burdened with chores and housework, and suffering endless abuse at her stepmother's hands, she finds solace when she ends up befriending a beautiful, 10-foot-long (3.0 m) fish in the lake. With golden eyes and scales, the fish is the reincarnation of her mother, who now watches out for her.

Angry that Yeh-Shen has found happiness, Jin kills the fish and serves it for dinner for herself and her daughter. Yeh-Shen is devastated until a spirit appears and tells her to bury the bones of the fish in pots at each corner of her bed. The spirit also tells her that whatever she needs will be granted if she talks to the bones.

The local spring festival takes place, where many young women will have the opportunity to meet potential suitors. Not wishing to spoil her own daughter's chances, Jin forces her stepdaughter to remain home and clean their cave-house. After her stepfamily has left, Yeh-Shen is visited by her mother's spirit again. Her mother tells her to dig up the pots containing the fish bones and Yeh-Shen finds fine clothes, including a cloak of kingfisher feathers, jewellery, and a pair of golden slippers to wear to the festival.

Yeh-Shen dons the clothes and goes to the festival by foot. She stays and enjoys herself until she realizes her stepmother may have recognized her and leaves, accidentally leaving behind a golden slipper. When she arrives home, she hides the clothes in the pots beneath her bed again. When her stepfamily returns, they discuss Jun-li's marriage prospects and also mention a mysterious maiden who appeared. They are unaware that it is Yeh-Shen they are speaking of.

The golden slipper is found and traded by various people until it reaches the hands of a nearby King. Fascinated by the shoe's small size, he issues a search to find the maiden whose foot will fit into the shoe and proclaims he will marry that girl. The shoe eventually reaches the cave-house of Yeh-Shen, Jun-li and her mother try to put on the shoe and fail. The shoe ends up fitting Yeh-Shen's foot perfectly.

In an attempt to dissuade the King from marrying Yeh-Shen, Jin declares that it was impossible for Yeh-Shen to have been at the festival. She saw the maiden who owns the golden slipper at the festival, the fine clothes she wore, and also mentions that Yeh-Shen was at home the entire time. Yeh-Shen proves her wrong by bringing out and putting the clothes she wore at the festival and the other golden slipper and the King, awed by Yeh-Shen's beauty, affirms that he will marry her, and she will become his chief wife in his palace. Jin makes a final attempt to dissuade the King from marrying her stepdaughter by accusing Yeh-Shen of stealing the maiden's golden shoe, but however, the King caught on and her evil plan was exposed. To punish Yeh-Shen's stepfamily for their cruelty and dishonesty, he forbids Yeh-Shen from bringing them to live with her. Jin and Jun-li were banished to a cave, where they spend the rest of their lives together until they are crushed to death by a shower of flying stones.

Adaptations

The novel Bound by Donna Jo Napoli is a retelling of this fairy tale.

Yeh-Shen: A Cinderella Story From China retold by Ai-Ling Louie and illustrated by Ed Young is well-known children's picture book adaptation of the fairy tale.

Yeh-Shen was also animated for the CBS Saturday Morning show, CBS Storybreak.

Source (edited): "http://en.wikipedia.org/wiki/Yeh-Shen:_A_Cinderella_Story_From_China"

Diamond Cut Diamond

Diamond Cut Diamond may refer to:
- Diamond Cut Diamond (fairy tale)
- *Diamond Cut Diamond (film)*, a British film

Source (edited): "http://en.wikipedia.org/wiki/Diamond_Cut_Diamond"

Jackal or Tiger?

Jackal or Tiger? is an Indian fairy tale. Andrew Lang included it in *The Olive Fairy Book*.

Synopsis

A king and queen, abed at night, heard a howl. The king thought it was a tiger, and the queen a jackal. They argued. The king said that if it were a jackal, he would leave the kingdom to her; if it were a tiger, he would send her away and marry another woman. Then he summoned the guards to settle it. The guards decided they had to agree with the king or get in trouble, so they said it was a tiger.

The king abandoned the queen in the forest. A farmer gave her shelter, and she gave birth to a son, Ameer Ali. When he was eighteen, Ameer Ali set out to have adventures. He shot at a pigeon and broke an old woman's pot, so he gave her the brass pot he carried, and fetched water for her. He briefly saw a beautiful young woman in her hut. In the morning, she told him that if he ever needed aid, to call the fairy of the forest. He thought only of the beautiful young woman.

He went to the king's palace and entered his service. One stormy night, a woman was heard wailing outside. The king ordered a servant to find out what it was, but the servant begged to be let off. Ameer Ali offered to go. He found a woman wailing beneath a gallows, though she was in reality an ogress. She told Ameer Ali that the body was her son's. When he tried to get it down for her, she tried to catch him, but he stabbed her and she fled, leaving behind an anklet. He told the king his story. The king gave the anklet to his proud and spoiled daughter.

She had two talking birds, a parrot and a starling. The starling thought the anklet became her. The parrot said her legs did not match. The princess demanded of her father a matching anklet. The king ordered Ameer Ali to find another within a month or die. With only a week left, Ameer Ali thought to call on the fairy of the forest. The beautiful young woman appeared. She told him to arrange wands, and then cut off her foot; the blood would make jewels. Then he would put back the foot and switch the wands, and she would be well again. Unwillingly, he obeyed her, and got the jewels. He was easily able to find someone to set them.

The starling admired the pair, but the parrot said she had all the beauty at one end. The princess demanded a necklace and bracelets from her father, and the king demanded them of Ameer Ali. By the same means, he had them made.

The parrot now complained that she dressed up for herself alone; she should marry. The princess told her father that she wanted to marry Ameer Ali. He agreed. Ameer Ali refused, and the king threw him into prison, although he thought his daughter should still marry, so he sent for men fit for a bridegroom and a royal heir.

The farmer joined the throng and made a petition: telling the king to remember that the tiger lived in the forest while the jackals hunted anywhere food could be found. He explained how he had found the queen and Ameer Ali was her son, and the king was ashamed of himself. He gave his throne to his son, who married the beautiful young fairy.

Source (edited): "http://en.wikipedia.org/wiki/Jackal_or_Tiger%3F"

The Fisher-Girl and the Crab

The Fisher-Girl and the Crab is an Indian fairy tale collected by Verrier Elwin in *Folk-Tales of Mahakoshal*; it comes from the Kuruk, a people living in Chitrakot, Bastar State.

Synopsis
A Kuruk couple had no children. They found a gourd by their rice field and started to eat it, but it begged them to cut gently. They found a crab inside it. The woman tied a basket to her belly, pretended to be pregnant, and then pretended to have given birth to the crab. In time, they married him off, but the girl did not like being married to a crab. She sneaked off when the parents and crab were asleep, but the crab sneaked ahead of her. He asked a banyan tree whose it was; it said it was his; he ordered it to fall down. He took out a human shape from inside it and put it on, putting his crab shape in the tree. The girl met him at a dance and gave him her ornaments. He went back before her and took on his crab shape again, and gave her her ornaments, which frightened her. She went to sneak out again but watched the crab. When he had put on the human shape, she asked the trees whose it was; it said it was hers; she ordered it to fall down and burned the crab shape. When her husband could not find her at the dance, he came back, and she jumped out, caught him, and took him home.

Commentary
Elwin noted that the crab is considered monogamous and an example of domestic fidelity.

Source (edited): "http://en.wikipedia.org/wiki/The_Fisher-Girl_and_the_Crab"

The Jogi's Punishment

The Jogi's Punishment is an Indian fairy tale, a Punjabi story collected by Major Campbell in Feroshepore. Andrew Lang included it in *The Lilac Fairy Book*.

Synopsis
A rajah made a jogi welcome in his city, building a house where he might receive guests. The rajah's only child was a beautiful daughter, who was betrothed to a neighboring prince. One day this daughter visited the jogi, who was instantly attracted to her. She guessed his intention and fled, and the jogi threw a lance after her, wounding her in the leg.

The next day, the jogi claimed to have been visited by a demon, which came disguised as a beautiful young woman but transformed into a hideous monster. The rajah had to find a beautiful young woman with a lance wound. When he did so, and realized it was his daughter, the jogi declared that his true daughter had been replaced in infancy by this evil spirit. The king made a chest, and they put the daughter in it and threw it in the river.

The next morning, her betrothed was hunting by the river and found the chest. He freed her and found that she was his betrothed. They married on the spot. The prince had a great monkey put in the chest in the princess's place, and the chest put back in the river. The jogi had his pupils retrieve it and then ordered them not to come into the room, whatever screams they heard. He took out a silken cord to strangle the princess. Shortly thereafter, they heard screams for help but did not enter. Eventually they did and found the jogi's body.

When the princess heard the jogi was dead, she made her peace with her father.

The King Who Would Be Stronger Than Fate

The King Who Would Be Stronger Than Fate is an Indian fairy tale, included by Andrew Lang in *The Brown Fairy Book*.

Synopsis

A king with a daughter once was lost while hunting and met a hermit, who prophesied that his daughter would marry a slave woman's son, who belonged to the king of the north. As soon as he left the forest, he sent an offer to the king of the north for the slave woman and her son. The other king made him a present of them. He took them into the forest and cut off the woman's head, and left the child there.

A widow who raised goats found that her best nanny-goat returned without a drop of milk. She followed the animal when it went to the child, and thought she had at least a son to look after her in her old age.

When the boy was grown, a peddler's donkey started to eat his mother's cabbages, and so he beat it and drove it out. The tale was borne to the peddler, with added claims that the boy had threatened to kill the peddler. The peddler complained to the king, who sent men to seize the boy. The old woman pled for his life, because she needed him to support her. The king, not believing that so old a woman could have so young a son, demanded to know where she had gotten him, and hearing the story, knew who the child was.

The king let him off if he joined the army. When the army life did not kill him, though he was sent on the most dangerous missions, and he proved a good soldier, he was enrolled in the king's bodyguard and saved him from an assassin. The king was obliged to make him an attendant, and in his missions for the king, he was continually attacked but always escaped. Finally, the king sent him with a message to a distant governor, who had charge of the princess. The mischievous princess was up and about while the rest of the castle slept in the heat of the day and found that the message was to kill the bearer of it. She substituted a letter ordering the governor to marry him to the princess.

The king, on receiving the news, abandoned his efforts to harm the boy.

Source (edited): "http://en.wikipedia.org/wiki/The_King_Who_Would_Be_Stronger_Than_Fate"

The Snake Prince

The Snake Prince is an Indian fairy tale, Punjabi story collected by Major Campbell Feroshepore. Andrew Lang included it in *The Olive Fairy Book*.

Synopsis

A poor woman, with nothing to eat, went to bathe. When she came out of the river, she found a poisonous snake in her pot. She took it home, so it would bite her and end her misery. When she opened the pot, she found a rich necklace. She sold it to the king. The king put it in a chest, but when he opened it to show the queen, he found a baby boy. He and the queen raised it as their son, and the old woman was the nurse. She spoke a little of how that boy came about.

The king had concluded with a neighboring king that his son should marry that king's daughter, and when the daughter came to marry, her mother warned her to ask about the magic. She refused to speak until he told her. He told her the story, that he was prince from far off who had been turned into a snake, and then he became a snake again. The princess mourned for the prince where he had vanished, and the snake came to her. He told that if she put bowls of milk and sugar in the four corners of the room, snakes would come, led by the Queen of the Snakes. If she stood in the queen's way, she could ask for her husband, but if she were frightened and did not, she could not have him back.

The princess did as he said, and won back her husband.

Source (edited): "http://en.wikipedia.org/wiki/The_Snake_Prince"

The Tiger, the Brahmin and the Jackal

an illustration of a variant of the tale

The Tiger, the Brahmin and the Jackal is a popular Indian fairy tale with a long history and many variants. A version was included in Joseph Jacobs' collection *Indian Fairy Tales*.

Synopsis

A brahmin passes a tiger in a trap. The tiger pleads for his release, promising not to eat the brahmin. The brahmin sets him free, but no sooner is the tiger free than he announces his intention to eat the brahmin.

The brahmin is horrified, and tells the tiger how unjust he is. They agree that they will ask the first three things they encounter to judge between them.

The first thing they encounter is a tree, who, having suffered at the hands of humankind, answers that the tiger should have his meal. Next a buffalo, exploited and then mistreated, feels it is only just that the brahmin should be eaten.

Finally they meet a jackal, who at first feigns incomprehension of what has happened and asks to see the trap. Once there he claims still not to understand. The tiger gets back in the trap to demonstrate, and the jackal quickly shuts him in, suggesting to the brahmin that they leave matters thus.

Variants

an illustration by John D. Batten for 1912 book by Joseph Jacobs.

There are more than a hundred versions of this tale spread across the world. In some the released animal is a crocodile, in some a snake, a tiger and others a wolf.

Some variants are very old, going back at least to the *Panchatantra* or *Fables of Bidpai* and the Jataka tales. In Europe it appeared some 900 years ago in the *Disciplina Clericalis* of Petrus Alphonsi, and later in the *Gesta Romanorum* and the *Directorium Vitae Humanae* of John of Capua. There are also modern illustrated versions of the tale, such as *The Tiger, the Brahmin & the Jackal* illustrated by David Kennett and *The Tiger and the Brahmin* illustrated by Kurt Vargo. Rabbit Ears Productions produced a video version of the last book, narrated by Ben Kingsley, with music by Ravi Shankar.

Source (edited): "http://en.wikipedia.org/wiki/The_Tiger,_the_Brahmin_and_the_Jackal"

Bawang Putih Bawang Merah

Bawang Putih Bawang Merah is one of the more famous of old Malay archipelago folktales, passed down orally through the generations. Like most Malay folktales, the story is laden with lessons regarding familial values, patience in the face of adversity, and that ultimately good will be rewarded and the evil will be punished.

The story centers on a pair of half-sisters named Bawang Putih and Bawang Merah. Bawang Putih is the Malay name for garlic, while Bawang Merah is the Malay name for onion or shallot. This naming convention is in the same vein as the Western fairy tale sisters Snow White and Rose Red although the previous do not get along as well. The use of these names for the female protagonist and her antagonist is symbolic of their physical similarity (both girls are beautiful) but have completely different personalities. Since the original folktale was passed on orally, different variations of the story exist. In some versions, Bawang Putih is the good and kind daughter, while Bawang Merah is the cruel and vindictive one. While in the original 1959 black and white Malay movie, it is the other way around, the shallot being waterly bringing tears to the eyes and garlic being pungent.

Story

The story takes place in a simple village household. The head of this family has two wives, and each wife has their own daughter. Bawang Merah and her mother are jealous of the attention the father gives Bawang Putih and her mother. When the father dies, Bawang Merah and her mother take charge of the household and bully Bawang Putih into servitude. Bawang Putih's mother stands up for her daughter but she soon dies prematurely, in some versions due to sickness and in some versions due to the intentional malice of Bawang Merah's mother.

With her biological mother and father dead, the gentle and obedient Bawang Putih is left alone to be tortured by her cruel stepmother and half-sister. Though Bawang Putih suffers, she is patient. One day, when she is out in the woods, she sees a pond containing a live fish. The fish is able to speak, and tells her that it is her mother who has come back to comfort her. Bawang Putih is overjoyed to be able to speak with her mother again, and secretly visits the pond whenever she can.

One day Bawang Merah sees Bawang Putih sneaking off and secretly follows her to the pond, where she witnesses Bawang Putih talking to the fish. After Bawang Putih leaves, Bawang Merah lures the fish to the surface of the pond and catches it. Bawang Merah and her mother kill the fish, cook it and feed it to Bawang Putih without telling her where it came from. Once Bawang Putih finishes eating, her stepmother and stepsister reveal where they obtained the fish. Bawang Putih is repulsed and filled with remorse over this revelation.

Bawang Putih gathers the fish bones and bury them in a small grave underneath a tree. When she visits the grave the next day, she is surprised to see that a beautiful swing has appeared from one of the tree's branches. When Bawang Putih sits in the swing and sings an old lullaby, it magically swings back and forth.

Bawang Putih continues to visit the magic swing whenever she can. One day, while she is on the magic swing, a Prince who is hunting nearby hears her song. He follows the sound of her voice, but before he approaches her, Bawang Putih realizes that she is not alone, she quickly runs back home.

The Prince and his advisors eventually find the home of Bawang Putih and Bawang Merah. (In some versions this happens immediately after the Prince's first sighting of Bawang Putih, but in other versions it happens after a long search made by the Prince's advisors). Bawang Merah's mother, seeing the opportunity, orders Bawang Putih to stay hidden in the kitchen. The Prince asks about the swing and the girl who sat in it. Bawang Merah's mother says that the girl he heard is her beautiful and talented daughter Bawang Merah. Though the Prince agrees that Bawang Merah is beautiful, he requests that she show him how she sang in the magical swing.

Bawang Merah and mother reluctantly follow the Prince and his advisors back to the magic swing. Bawang Merah sits in the swing and attempts to sing so that it will move, but she cannot. The Prince, now angry, ordered Bawang Merah's mother to tell the truth. Bawang Merah's mother is forced to confess that she has another daughter hidden in her house.

The Prince brings Bawang Putih back to the swing, and as she had done many times before, the magic swing starts moving as soon as she begins singing. The Prince is overjoyed and asks Bawang Putih to marry him. She agrees and they live happily ever after.

Adaptations

- *Bawang Putih Bawang Merah*, 1959 Malaysian live-action musical, starring Latifah Omar as a good Bawang Merah, Umi Kalthom as a bad Bawang Putih, and Mustapha Maarof as the Prince. In this film, the adaptation is twisted where Bawang Putih as a bad stepsister, whilst Bawang Merah as a good sister.
- *Bawang Putih Bawang Merah*, 1986 made-for-television Malaysian remake of the 1959 version.
- *Putih*, 2001 Malaysian animated musical, starring the voices of Erra Fazira as Putih, Raja Azura as Merah and M. Nasir as Putera Aftus.
- *Bawang Putih Bawang Merah*, 2006 Indonesian television serial starring Revalina S. Temat as a good Bawang Putih and Nia Ramadhani as a bad Bawang Merah.
- *Bawang Putih Bawang Merah: The Movie*, 2007 Indonesian film starring Laudya Cynthia Bella, Eva Anindita, Nana Khairina and Ferry Irawan.

Source (edited): "http://en.wikipedia.org/wiki/Bawang_Putih_Bawang_Merah"

Damarwulan

Depiction of the hero **Damarwulan** in a wayang kulit puppet.

Damarwulan is a Javanese cultural hero who appears in a cycle of stories used in the performance of wayang klitik, as well as Langendriya (female dance-opera) and ketoprak (popular theater). These stories tell of the struggles between the Majapahit and Blambangan kingdoms, in which Damarwulan gains honor. The stories are especially popular in East Java.

Origin

The Damarwulan legend is associated with the Majapahit court at the time of the queen Suhita, at which time there was a war with Blambangan. However, the names of the characters Damar Wulan ("radiance of the moon") and Menak Jingga ("red knight") suggest that it may incorporate elements of an older sun-moon myth. It is uncertain when the story was first recorded and by whom.

Characters

- Prabu Kenya, the maiden queen of Majapahit
- Patih Logender, her prime minister
- Layang Seta and Layang Kumitir, the prime minister's sons
- Dewi Anjasmara, the prime minister's daughter
- Damarwulan, the prime minister's nephew, raised away from court by his grandfather
- Menak Jingga, the King of Blambangan, a vassal of Majapahit
- Dewi Wahita and Dewi Puyengan, princesses held captive by Menak Jingga
- Sabdapalon and Nayagenggong, Damarwulan's servants

Synopsis

Depiction of the villain **Menak Jingga** in a wayang kulit puppet.

Damarwulan is a prince by birth, a nephew of the prime minister, Patih Logender, but was raised in the hermitage of his grandfather. Following his grandfather's advice, he goes to the Majapahit court seeking employment. His cousins, the prime minister's sons, mistreat him when he arrives. Patih Logender, not wanting him to compete with his own sons, assigns him as grass-cutter and stableboy. Though he is stripped of his fine garments, he still has his striking beauty. Rumors of this beauty eventually reach Anjasmara, the prime minister's daughter. She seeks him out secretly and they fall in love and are clandestinely married. One night, Anjasmara's brothers overhear voices in her chamber. They break in and try to kill Damarwulan, but he is able to overcome them. They flee to their father, who orders that Damarwulan be executed. Anjasmara pleas for her lover, and he doesn't execute Damarwulan, but imprisons the pair.

Meanwhile, Menak Jingga has wrote a letter to the queen asking for her hand. When the queen rejects him, he declares war on the Majapahit kingdom. He is successful in dispatching Majapahit's allies, and finally the kingdom is threatened by his forces directly. In distress, the queen announces that whoever kills Menak Jingga and brings her his head can have her hand. Worried when no saviors present themselves, she has a divine revelation that a young knight named Damarwulan can overcome him. She orders Patih Logender to release him from jail and send him forth on his mission.

Damarwulan, accompanied by his servants, makes his way to Blambangan. Arriving at night, he steals into the gardens and manages to overhear a conversation at the pavilion between two resentful captive princesses. Damarwulan enters the pavilion and confides in them, and, enraptured by his beauty, they become devoted to him. At this time, Menak Jingga decides to visit the princesses, and discovers Damarwulan. They fight, but Damarwulan is unable to hurt Menak Jingga, and, severely wounded, appears to die. Menak Jingga leaves, ordering his servants to guard the body. However, they fall asleep, and the two princesses carry him away, revive him, and explain to the secret of Menak Jingga's magic invulnerability, a club of yellow iron kept behind his headrest. If the king is hit on his left temple with this club, he will die. Risking their lives for the sake of their lover, the princesses manage to steal the club while the king is asleep. A second battle between Menak Jingga and Damarwulan follows, in which Damarwulan manages to behead the king. Successful, he returns to Majapahit, but the prime minister's sons ambush him outside the palace, killing him and presenting Menak Jingga's head to the queen. However, a hermit revives Damarwulan, and the queen learns what happened. In a final battle, Damarwulan defeats his cousins, is crowned King of Majapahit, and is permitted to retain Anjasmara as his other wife.

Source (edited): "http://en.wikipedia.org/wiki/Damarwulan"

Panji (prince)

Raden Panji Asmoro Bangun searching for his lost wife, Dewi Sekartaji

Panji (formerly **Pandji**) was a legendary prince in East Java, Indonesia. His life has formed the basis of a cycle of Javanese stories. Along with the Ramayana and Mahabharata, this cycle is the basis of various poems and a genre of wayang (shadow puppetry) known as *wayang gedog* -- "gedog" meaning "mask". Panji tales have also spread from East Java to be a fertile source for literature and drama throughout Malaya, Thailand, and Cambodia.

Characters and names

Panji and the other characters in the Panji cycle appear with various names in different versions of the tales. Other names for Panji include Raden Panji, Raden Inu, Inu (of) Koripan, Ino (or Hino) Kartapati, Cekel Wanengpati, and Kuda Wanengpati of Janggala. Panji also found as a name of Prince of the monarchy in Tabanan, rules by Shri Arya Kenceng on 1414 (Babad Arya Tabanan.) In Thailand, he is called Enau (Thai: อิเหนา) or Enau (of) Kurepan, or Raden Montree.

Panji is the prince of Kuripan (Koripan) or Janggala. He is usually depicted in an unadorned helmetlike rounded cap. The mask for Panji has a smooth white or green face; narrow, elongated eyes; a straight and pointed nose; and delicate, half-open lips.

Panji is engaged to be married to Candra Kirana (also known as Sekartaji), the princess of Daha (Kediri), when she mysteriously disappears on the eve of the wedding. Later in the story, she is sometimes called Kuda Narawangsa when she appears disguised as a man. Panji's principal adversary is Klono (Kelana Tunjung Seta), a ferocious king who desires Candra Kirana and tries to destroy Daha to get her. Other common characters are Gunung Sari (Candra Kirana's brother), Ragil Kuning or Dewi Onengan (Panji's sister married to Gunung Sari), Wirun, Kartala and Andaga (relatives and companions of Panji).

Synopsis

Balinese painting of Prince Panji meeting three women in the jungle

There are many differing versions and episodes of the overall story. In one version, The main story of Panji tells about the romance between Prince Panji and Princess Kirana; the Panji search for his long lost bride.

Smaradhana

The kakawin Smaradhana originally was the work of the poet Mpu Dharmaja in early 12th century. However later incorporated as the prelude of Panji tales. The story tells about the disappearance of Kamajaya and his wife, Kamaratih from svargaloka because being burnt by the fire of Shiva. The spirit of Kamajaya and Kamaratih was fell upon the earth incarnated several times as the mortal among human beings. The main character of Panji cyle; Prince Panji and Princess Kirana is the notable incarnation of Kamajaya and Kamaratih on earth. These are several episodes of the compilation of Panji story:

Chandra Kirana

The tales of Chandra Kirana (sometimes called the tales of Dewi Anggraeni) is a tragic love story, the prequel of the main Panji story. The story began with the arranged marriage between Prince Panji Asmoro Bangun, and Princess Chandra Kirana from twin neighboring kingdoms of Kediri and Janggala. The dynastic marriage was meant to unite the once single kingdom under one dynasty as the means of peace agreement. During his early youth, the prince of Jenggala love to travel the country, visit some ashrams and hermitages and learn from various wise Brahmins and rishis across the kingdom. However during his stays in one of a remote hermitage, the prince fell in love with a beautiful commoner girl, Dewi Anggraeni. The prince married Anggraeni and took her home to the palace in the capital city of Jenggala. The marriage of a prince with the commoner girl uproared royal court of both Jenggala and Kediri. The angered Kediri envoys push the commitment of Jenggala to keep their promise on the arranged dynastic marriage, they threatened to wage the war if the marriage failed. However the love-struck Prince did not want to fulfilled his royal duty and refused to marry Kirana. To avoid the war, the elders of royal house plotted an assassination to kill Dewi Anggraeni.

Both Panji and Anggraeni was separated and tricked by being told to meet each other. Actually Anggraeni was brought by royal troops deep into a forest to be murdered. After she learned that the action was meant to avoid war and bloodshed between two kingdoms, the poor girl willingly gave up her life and sacrifice herself. After Panji learn about the death of Anggraeni, the prince went amok, fell unconscious and finally lost his mind. The prince went insane, suffer amnesia and wracking havoc across the kingdoms; attacking various villages authorities, lords, and bandits. Meanwhile in Kediri, Princess Kirana that learn about fate of her future husband, decided to go out from the palace to find and help him. Later princess Kirana disguised as a man involved in a battle with Panji and finally managed to cure the Prince from insanity. Surprisingly Princess Kirana looks exactly like the late Anggraeni, as actually they both was incarnated by the same spirit, Kamaratih, the goddess of love. Panji and Kirana later united in marriage and life happily ever after.

Panji Semirang

The episode of Panji Semirang tell another version of the story. The story began with the disappearance of Candra Kirana from the palace. After Candra Kirana disappears, a princess who claims to be Candra Kirana, though different in appearance, attempts to console Prince Panji, and alleges that she was carried off by Durga, and will regain her original appearance as soon as they are married. Panji orders preparations for the wedding resume, not knowing that the consoler is in reality a demon-princess who wants Panji for herself.

Meanwhile, the true Candra Kirana is alone in the forest, advised by gods that she must return to the palace disguised as a man to be reunited with Panji. She does so, discovers the wedding plans to the false Candra Kirana, writes a letter to Panji revealing the true situation, and vanishes. Upon discovering this, Panji rushes to search for his love while his courtiers kill the demonic impostor.

Panji undergoes many adventures, staying in forests with hermits, working as a servant in different palaces, always searching for traces of his lost bride. Candra Kirana, meanwhile, continues her male disguise, undergoes her own set of adventures, and ends up as the king of Bali. In the climax of the story, Panji and Candra Kirana unknowingly oppose each other on the battlefield. There, as witnesses are ordered to leave, she confides to her opponent that she is the bride of Panji, and that the disguise was assumed because of a command of the gods that she could win back her prince only in a face-to-face combat where his blood is made to flow. They fight with swords and arrows, but she is unable to harm him until she resorts to her hairpin. Panji is wounded, reveals his identity, and they are happily reunited.

Ande Ande Lumut

The episode Ande Ande Lumut told another version of the union between Prince Kusumayuda and Kleting Kuning, the youngest of four sisters, all are the daughters of a widow in a village within the Prince Kusumayuda's father domain. The widow daughters are named according to colors; from the oldest Kleting Abang (Kleting Merah/Red Kleting), Kleting Biru (Blue Kleting), Kleting Ijo (Green Kleting), and Kleting Kuning (Yellow Kleting). All of Kleting Kuning's older sisters are jealous because Kleting Kuning is very beautiful. Kleting Kuning actually was an adopted daughter, she is actually the missing princess of Janggala kingdom, later known as Dewi Candrakirana. Prince Kusumayuda always remember the beautiful princess that betrothed to him years ago, his future consort the future queen of Banyuarum kingdom. Unfortunately they were separated as the princess is missing.

Several years later a rich and handsome eligible bachelor named Ande Ande Lumut declared that he is searching for a bride to be married. Many girls across the kingdom are smitten and interested to be his wife, including Kleting Kuning's sisters. However Kleting Kuning was not interested since she always remember her true love Prince Kusumayuda. However a magical crane bird told Kleting Kuning to participate in this event since her true fate is waiting. All of the girls are all dressed up beautifully, put on their make up and marched towards Ande Ande Lumut's house. However her stepmother ordered Kleting Kuning not to dressed up and even disguised her in ugly and dirty clothes, in favour of her oown daughters to win the bachelor's heart. She only gave her a *sapu lidi* (broom made of coconut leaf spines) in order to make Kleting Kuning looks like a poor servant, however actually it was a magical broom.

In their journey, the girls have to cross a large river without any ferry services. The river was guarded by a giant freshwater crab named Yuyu Kangkang. Yuyu Kangkang offered to take the girls crossed the river rides upon its back, in return for a kiss. In order to reach Ande Ande Lumut's house as fast as possible, hastely the girls agreed on this condition and allowed Yuyu Kangkang to kiss them. Kleting Kuning arrived late on the river bank where Yuyu Kangkang awaits and again Yuyu Kangkang offers its service for a kiss. Of course Kleting Kuning whom always uphold her modesty and chastity refuse its offer. Yuyu Kangkang angered with Kleting Kuning refusal and tried to eat her. In defense Kleting Kuning hit the river with her broom and magically all the water in the river is dried, so Kuning able to cross the river safely. Yuyu Kangkang is very scared and beg for her mercy and forgiveness to return the river, its home, as it was before. All the girls including Kleting Kuning's sisters reach Ande Ande Lumut's house and greeted by Ande Ande Lumut's mother. Although the girls are pretty, Ande Ande Lumut refused all of them because he can detect the smelly pungent fishy kiss of Yuyu Kangkang on them. Finally Kleting Kuning arrived, she looks dirty and ugly. However Ande Ande Lumut received her as he can see the true beauty beneath and he knows that Kleting Kuning is the long lost princess. At that time Kleting Kuning realized that Ande Ande Lumut is actually Prince Kusumayuda himself. They are reunited, married and life happily ever after.

Keong Emas

Another episode is the sequel of the main story. The tale of Keong Emas took place after the union of Panji Asmoro Bangun and Sekartaji in a marriage. There is several versions of the tale. The story began with Sekartaji being magically transformed into a golden snail. The golden snail was saved and kept as a pet by a poor widow fisherwoman named Mbok Rondo. Magically Sekartaji able to turned back into her human form for some period and she paid back the widow's kindness by cooked her delicious dishes and cleaned her house. The curious Mbok Rondo finally learn that the snail is a princess and she broke the snail shell and thus undo the magic spell. Sekartaji was adopted as the widow's daughter and finally reunited with her husband, Panji Asmoro Bangun.

Origin
In these romances, he is said to do deeds traditionally ascribed to mythical ancestors, and it has also been conjectured that the basis of the story reflects an ancient sun and moon myth. Some details of Panji may also be based on Kameçvara, a twelfth-century Javanese king of Kediri. While the details of Panji's consort, Chandra Kirana, was based on queen Çri Kirana. The curious thing is, the kingdoms in the tale was switched from the historical kingdoms. In the tale Panji was said to be the prince of Janggala, while the historic Kameçvara was the prince of Kediri. Vice versa, in the tale, Chandra Kirana was said to be the princess of Kediri, while the actual historic Çri Kirana was the princess of Janggala. In the Surakarta court poet Ranggawarsita's genealogy *Pustaka Radja Mada*, the Javanese kings, including Panji, are considered the descendents of the Pandawas of the Mahabharata.

Appearances in art and literature
Scenes from the Panji cycles appear in the narrative reliefs of the walls of East Javanese candi from the 13th century, where they are presented gracefully, naturalistically and delicately, in contrast to wayang style.

Sunan Giri is credited, along with other innovations in wayang, with the creation of wayang gedog in 1553, to enact the Panji stories. Wayang kulit performances of the Panji cycle are in general the same as in performances of the *wayang purwa* (those based on the Indian epics); however, because of their material they are considered less significant. In addition, their headdresses are simpler and the garment worn on the lower body is based on Javanese court dress Plots based on the Panji cycle are also common in East Javanese wayang klitik (using wooden puppets), in West Javanese wayang golek (using three-dimensional rod puppets), and in wayang beber (stories depicted pictorially on scrolls). It is also the principal basis of the stories used in wayang topeng (masked dance-pantomime). In Bali, where the cycle is known as *Malat*, the story is performed in the Gambuh plays and in the operatic Arja.
Source (edited): "http://en.wikipedia.org/wiki/Panji_(prince)"

Bunbuku Chagama

Illustration of Bunbuku Chagama by Tsukioka Yoshitoshi, 1889-1892.

Bunbuku Chagama (Japanese: ぶんぶく茶釜) is a Japanese folktale about a raccoon-dog, or tanuki, that uses its shapeshifting powers to reward its rescuer for his kindness.

Story
Bunbuku Chagama roughly translates to "happiness bubbling over like a tea pot." The story tells of a poor man who finds a tanuki caught in a trap. Feeling sorry for the animal, he sets it free. That night, the tanuki comes to the poor man's house to thank him for his kindness. The tanuki transforms itself into a chagama (tea kettle) and tells the man to sell him for money.

The man sells the tanuki-teapot to a monk, who takes it home and, after scrubbing it harshly, sets it over the fire to boil water. Unable to stand the heat, the tanuki teapot sprouts legs and, in its half-transformed state, makes a run for it.

The tanuki returns to the poor man with another idea. The man would set up a 'roadside attraction' (a little circus-like setup) and charge admission for people to see a teapot walking a tightrope. The plan works, and each gains something good from the other—the man is no longer poor and the tanuki has a new friend and home.

In a variant of the story, the tanuki-teapot does not run and returns to its transformed state. The shocked monk decides to leave the teapot as an offering to the poor temple where he lives, choosing not to use it for making tea again. The temple eventually becomes famous for its supposed dancing teapot.

Cultural impact
An animated movie based on the tale was produced in 1928 by Yokohama Cinema Shoukai. There is also a reference to this story in Studio Ghibli's 1994 animated film Pom Poko.

A character in the manga To Love-Ru is seen holding the book and commenting that she is taking an interest in Japanese folklore.
Source (edited): "http://en.wikipedia.org/wiki/Bunbuku_Chagama"

Hanasaka Jiisan

Hanasaka Jiisan is a Japanese fairy tale. Algernon Bertram Freeman-Mitford collected it in *Tales of Old Japan*, as **The Story of the Old Man Who Made Withered Trees to Blossom**. Andrew Lang included it, as **The Envious Neighbor**, in *The Violet Fairy Book*, listing his sources as *Japanische Marchen*.

Synopsis

An old childless couple loved their dog. One day, it dug in the garden, and they found a box of gold pieces there. A neighbor thought the dog must be able to find treasure, and managed to borrow the dog. When it dug in his garden, there were only bones, and he killed it. He told the couple that the dog had just dropped dead. They grieved and buried it under the fig tree where they had found the treasure. One night, the dog's master dreamed that the dog told him to chop down the tree and make a mortar from it. He told his wife, who said they must do as the dog asked. When they did, the rice put into the mortar turned into gold. The neighbor borrowed it, but the rice turned to foul-smelling berries, and he and his wife smashed and burned the mortar.

That night, in a dream, the dog told his master to take the ashes and sprinkle them on certain cherry trees. When he did, the cherry trees came into bloom, and the Daimyo, passing by, marveled and gave him many gifts. The neighbor tried to do the same, but the ashes blew into the Daimyo's eyes, so he threw him into prison; when he was let out, his village would not let him live there anymore, and he could not, with his wicked ways, find a new home.

Source (edited): "http://en.wikipedia.org/wiki/Hanasaka_Jiisan"

Issun-bōshi

Issun-bōshi from Otogizōshi

The **One-Inch Boy** (一寸法師 **Issun-bōshi**; sometimes translated into English as "Little One Inch") is the subject of a fairy tale from Japan. This story can be found in old Japanese illustrated book, Otogizōshi, and has been various forms around the world and is similar to the tradition of Tom Thumb in English folklore.

Synopsis

The story begins with an old, childless couple who live alone. The old woman wishes for a child, despite her old age, "Please, please let us have a child, no matter how small." Eventually, a son was born to them. But small indeed was the child--no larger than a grown man's fingertip. They named the miniature child Issun-bōshi (Issun is a measure of approximately 3 centimeters. Bōshi means son). The child, despite being incredibly small, is treated well by his parents. One day, the boy realizes he will never grow, so he goes on a trip to seek his place in the world. Fancying himself a miniature samurai, Issun-bōshi is given a sewing needle for a sword, a soup bowl for a boat, and chopsticks for oars.

He sails down river to the city, where he petitions for a job with the government and goes to the home of a wealthy daimyo, whose daughter is an attractive princess. He is scorned for his height, but nevertheless given the job of accompanying the princess as her playmate. While they travel together, they are suddenly attacked by an oni, who deals with the pesky boy by swallowing him. The boy defeats the Oni by pricking him from within with his needle/sword. The Oni spits out Issun-boshi and drops the magical Uchide's Mallet as he runs away. As a reward for his bravery, the princess uses the power of the mallet to grow him to full size. Issun-bōshi and the princess remain close companions and eventually wed.

Appearances in other media

- *Gougou Sentai Boukenger*, a Japanese television series, has an episode ("Task 21: Uchide's Mallet") in which the hammer is a Precious.
- Issun-bōshi was the basis for one of the three OVAs based on the Mario series released in 1989.
- In the video game *Ōkami*, the character Issun is based on the one-inch boy. Uchide's Mallet (labeled as "Lucky Mallet") also appears in the game, although it is used to shrink the protagonist, a wolf avatar of the Shinto sun god Okami Amaterasu, to Issun's size, rather than the other way around. His form as seen through the first part of the game leads the player to believe he is some sort of insect (despite his adamant insistence otherwise), but he bears a resemblance to a one-inch boy during the portion of the game spent at Issun's size. Later it is revealed that he belongs to a race of tiny wood sprites called Poncles, who all appear as he does.
- In the video game *Secret of Mana*, there is a hammer called the "Midget Mallet" which grows and shrinks the user.
- In the *Final Fantasy series* of video games, the "Mini" status ailment can be cured using a "Mallet".
- In the video game *The World Ends with You*, there is a hammer called the *"Lucky Mallet"*.
- In the video game Mario & Luigi: Bowser's Inside Story, Luigi can use the mallet to shrink Mario, which may be referencing the One Inch

Boy or may be influenced by it. Source (edited): "http://en.wikipedia.org/wiki/Issun-b%C5%8Dshi"

Kachi-kachi Yama

Kachi-Kachi Yama (Japanese: かちかち山, *kachi-kachi* being an onomatopoeia of the sound a fire makes and *yama* meaning "mountain", roughly translates to "Fire-Crackle Mountain"), is one of the few Japanese folktales in which a tanuki is the villain, rather than the boisterous, well-endowed alcoholic.

Story

The trouble-making tanuki

As the story goes, a man caught a troublesome tanuki in his fields, and tied it to a tree to kill and cook it later. When the man left for town, the tanuki cried and begged the man's wife who was making some mochi, to set him free, promising he would help her. The wife freed the animal, only to have it turn on her and kill her. The tanuki then planned a foul trick.

Using its shapeshifting abilities, the tanuki disguised itself as the wife and cooked a soup, using the dead woman's flesh. When the man came home, the tanuki served him the soup. After the meal, the tanuki reverted to its original appearance and revealed its treachery before running off and leaving the poor man in shock and grief.

Enter the rabbit

The couple had been good friends with a rabbit that lived nearby. The rabbit approached the man and told him that it would avenge his wife's death. Pretending to befriend the tanuki, the rabbit instead tortured it through various means, from dropping a bee's nest on it to 'treating' the stings with a peppery poultice that burned.

The title of the story comes from the especially painful trick that the rabbit played. While the tanuki was carrying a heavy load of kindling on his back to make a campfire for the night, he was so burdened that he did not immediately notice when the rabbit set fire to the kindling. Soon, the crackling sound reached its ears and it asked the rabbit what the sound was. "It is Kachi-Kachi Yama" the rabbit replied. "We are not far from it, so it is no surprise that you can hear it!". Eventually, the fire reached the tanuki's back, burning it badly, but without killing it.

Boat of mud

The tanuki challenged the rabbit to a life or death contest to prove who was the better creature. They were each to build a boat and race across a lake in them. The rabbit carved its boat out of a fallen tree trunk, but the foolish tanuki made a boat of mud.

The two competitors were evenly matched at first, but the tanuki's mud boat began dissolving in the middle of the lake. As the tanuki was failing in its struggle to stay afloat, the rabbit proclaimed its friendship with the human couple, and that this was the tanuki's punishment for its horrible deeds.

Variations

There are other versions that alter some details of the story, such as the severity of what the tanuki did to the woman and how the tanuki got the mud boat.
Source (edited): "http://en.wikipedia.org/wiki/Kachi-kachi_Yama"

Momotarō

Bisque doll of Momotarō

Momotarō (桃太郎) is a popular hero from Japanese folklore. His name literally means *Peach Tarō*; as Tarō is a common Japanese boy's name, it is often translated as *Peach Boy*. *Momotarō* is also the title of various books, films, and other works that portray the tale of this hero.

Story

According to the present form of the tale (dating to the Edo period), Momotarō came to Earth inside a giant peach, which was found floating down a river by an old, childless woman who was washing clothes there. The woman and her husband discovered the child when they tried to open the peach to eat it. The child explained that he had been sent by Heaven to be their son. The couple named him Momotarō, from *momo* (peach) and *tarō* (eldest son in the family).

Years later, Momotarō left his parents to fight a band of marauding oni (demons or ogres) on a distant island. En route, Momotarō met and befriended a talking dog, monkey, and pheasant, who agreed to help him in his quest. At the island, Momotarō and his animal friends penetrated the demons' fort and beat the band of demons into surrendering. Momotarō and his new friends returned home with the demons' plundered treasure and the demon chief as a captive. Momotarō and his family lived comfortably from then on.

Momotarō is strongly associated with

Okayama, and his tale may have its origins there. The demon island (Onigashima (鬼ヶ島)) of the story is sometimes associated with Megijima Island, an island in the Seto Inland Sea near Takamatsu, due to the vast manmade caves found on that island.

Variants

There are a few variants to the story, depending on geographical region. Some say Momotaro floated by in a box, a white peach, or a red peach. Stories from Shikoku and Chugoku region muddy the distinction with characters from another folk story, the Monkey-Crab Battle that Momotaro took with him allies to Oni Island, namely a bee (蜂 *hachi*), a crab (蟹 *kani*), a mill stone (臼 *usu*), a chestnut (栗 *kuri*), and a cowpie (牛の糞 *ushi no hun*). In old days, all these animals and objects were believed to possess spirits and could move by their own will. The cowpie was sometimes given the honorific *dono* (殿). This was to appease the cowpie spirit, so as it won't move to be under you when you stumble or take a step.

Momotarō's song

Statue of Momotaro outside of Okayama Train Station

The popular children's song about Momotarō titled *Momotarō-san no Uta* (*Momotarō's Song*) was first published in 1911. One version of it is included below with romanization and translation.

« Momotarō-san no uta » 桃太郎さんの歌

Momotarō-san, momotarō-san (Momotarō, Momotarō) 桃太郎さん、桃太郎さん

Okoshi ni tsuketa kibidango (Those millet dumplings on your waist) お腰につけたきびだんご

Hitotsu watashi ni kudasai na? (Won't you give me one?) 一つ私に下さいな!

Agemashō, agemashō (I'll give you one, I'll give you one) あげましょう、あげましょう

Kore kara oni no seibatsu ni (From now, on a quest to conquer the ogres) これから鬼の征伐に

Tsuite kuru nara agemashō (If you come with me, I'll give one to you) ついてくるならあげましょう

World War II

Momotaro was an immensely popular figure during World War II, appearing in many wartime films and cartoons.

Source (edited): "http://en.wikipedia.org/wiki/Momotar%C5%8D"

My Lord Bag of Rice

The Dragon Princess and Fujiwara no Hidesato, Utagawa Kuniyoshi 1845.

Fujiwara no Hidesato shooting the giant centipede, Tsukioka Yoshitoshi 1890.

My Lord Bag of Rice or Japanese **Tawara Tōda** (俵藤太 "Rice-bag Tōda") is a fairy tale about a hero who kills the giant centipede Seta to help a Japanese dragon princess, and is rewarded in her underwater Ryūgū-jō 龍宮城 "dragon palace castle".

The 1711 *Honchō kwaidan koji* 本朝怪談故事 contains the best-known version of this Japanese myth about the warrior Fujiwara no Hidesato. There is a Shinto shrine near the Seta Bridge at Lake Biwa where people worship Tawara Tōda 俵藤太 "Rice-bag Tōda" (a pun between *tawara* "straw rice-bag; straw barrel" and the Japanese name Tawara 田原).

In olden times, when Fujiwara no Hidesato (who lived in the first half of the tenth century) crossed the bridge, a big serpent lay across it. The hero, however, was not at all afraid, and calmly stepped over the monster which at once disappeared into the water and returned in the shape of a beautiful woman. Two thousand years, she said, she had lived under this bridge, but never had she seen such a brave man as he. For this reason she requested him to destroy her enemy, a huge centipede, which had killed her sons and grandsons. Hidesato promised her to do so and, armed with a bow and arrows, awaited the centipede on the bridge. There came from the top of Mt. Mikami two enormous lights, as big as the light of two hundred torches. These were the centipede's eyes, and Hidesato sent three arrows in that direction, whereupon the lights were extinguished and the monster died. The dragon woman, filled with joy and gratitude, took the hero with her to the splendid Dragon-palace, where she regaled him with delicious dishes and rewarded him with a piece of silk, a sword, an armour, a temple bell and a bag (tawara) of rice. She said, that there would always be silk left as long as he lived, however much he might cut from it; and the bag of rice would never be empty.

Hidesato subsequently donated this bell to Mii-dera temple at Mount Hiei but it was stolen by a priest from rival Enryaku-ji temple. He threw it into a valley after it spoke to him, and when the cracked bell was returned to Mii-dera, a small snake (the dragon) used its tail to repair the damage. The 14th-century *Taiheiki* records an earlier version of this legend about Hidesato, set during the Genpei War, but instead of the dragon turning into a beautiful woman, it transforms into a "strange small man" – the Dragon King himself.

This Lord Bag of Rice fable is included in *Japanese Fairy Tales* by Yei Theodora Ozaki and *A Book of Dragons* by Ruth Manning-Sanders.

Source (edited): "http://en.wikipedia.org/wiki/My_Lord_Bag_of_Rice"

Schippeitaro

Schippeitaro is a Japanese fairy tale. Andrew Lang included it in *The Violet Fairy Book,* listing his source as *Ja-*

panische Marchen.

Synopsis

A young warrior wandered the land in search of adventure. One day, in the forest, he slept in a chapel; he was woken at midnight by ferocious yowls from cats, who were dancing and yelling, and some were saying, "Do not tell Schippeitaro!" He went on and found a village where he heard a woman lamenting and calling for help. He was told that every year they had to sacrifice a maiden to the spirit of the mountain, and this year, this was the woman. She was put in a cask, and the cask would put in the chapel where he had slept. He asked after Schippeitaro and heard it was the dog of the prince's overseer, living nearby. The warrior went to this man and persuaded him to lend him the dog. He brought it to the cask, freed the woman, and put the dog in her place. The cask was brought to the chapel, and the cats came. A huge black cat opened the cask, and Schippeitaro killed it, and then, with the warrior, several others before they fled. He brought Schippeitaro back to his owner in the morning, and every year a feast was held in honor of the warrior and Schippeitaro.

Source (edited): "http://en.wikipedia.org/wiki/Schippeitaro"

Shita-kiri Suzume

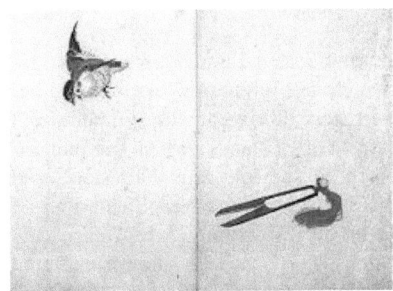

Katsushika Hokusai ukiyo-e

Shita-kiri Suzume (舌切り雀 *shi-takirisuzume*), translated literally into "**Tongue-Cut Sparrow**", is a traditional Japanese fable telling of a kind old man, his avaricious wife and an injured sparrow. The story explores the effects of greed, friendship and jealousy on the characters.

Andrew Lang included it as **The Sparrow with the Slit Tongue** in *The Pink Fairy Book*.

The basic form of the tale is common throughout the world.

The story

An old man went on his usual hike into the mountains to cut timber one morning and came upon an injured sparrow crying for help. Feeling sorry for the creature, the man takes it back to his home and feeds it some rice to try to help it recover. His wife, being very greedy and ill-natured, is annoyed that he would waste precious food on such a filthy little thing as the sparrow. The old man, however, continued caring for the bird.

The man had to return to the mountain one day and left the bird in the care of the old woman, who had no intention of feeding it. After her husband left, she went out fishing. While she was gone, the sparrow got into some starch that was left out and eventually ate it all. The old woman was so outraged upon her return that she cut out the bird's tongue, sending it flying back into the mountains from whence it came.

The old man went searching for the bird and, with the help of other sparrows, found his way into a bamboo grove in which the sparrow's inn was located. A multitude of sparrows greeted him and led him to his friend, the little sparrow he saved. The others brought him food and sang and danced for him.

Upon his departure, they presented him with a choice of a large basket or a small basket as a prize. Being old, he chose the small basket since he figured it would be the least heavy. When he arrived home, he opened the basket and an enormous amount of treasure was found inside. The wife, finding out there was a larger basket, ran to the inn in the hope of getting more treasure for herself. She chose the larger basket but was warned not to open it before getting home.

Such was her greed that she could not resist opening the basket on the way home. Much to her surprise, the box was full of ogres, snakes and other monsters. They scared her so badly that she tumbled all the way down the mountain, presumably to her death.

Themes

- The purity of friendship overcomes the evil of greed and jealousy.
- Greed only leads one to one's own demise.

Variants

The tale is classified as Aarne-Thompson type 480, "The Kind and the Unkind Girls." Others of this type include *Diamonds and Toads*, *Mother Hulda*, *The Three Heads in the Well*, *Father Frost*, *The Three Little Men in the Wood*, *The Enchanted Wreath*, *The Old Witch* and *The Two Caskets*. Literary variants include *The Three Fairies* and *Aurore and Aimée*.

In modern culture

In the Capcom game Ōkami, there is a hidden inn inhabited and run by sparrows, as well as an elderly couple who capture and plan to eat one of the sparrows. This is an obvious reference to the tale, though the nature of the husband has been changed.

Source (edited): "http://en.wikipedia.org/wiki/Shita-kiri_Suzume"

The Boy Who Drew Cats

"**The Boy Who Drew Cats**" is a Japanese fairy tale collected by Lafcadio Hearn in *Japanese Fairy Tales*.

Synopsis

A farmer and his wife had many children; the youngest son was too small and weak, and spent all his time drawing cats instead of doing his chores. So, they took him to the temple to become a priest. He learned quickly, but he drew cats everywhere. The old priest finally said he could not be a priest, though he might be an artist, and sent him away with the advice to avoid large places at night, and keep to small ones. He decided to go to a big temple nearby and ask them to take him on.

The temple had been deserted, because a goblin had driven the priests away, and warriors who went against it were never seen again. A light burned at the temple at night, so when the boy arrived, he went in. He saw some big white screens and painted cats on them. Then he went to sleep, but, since the temple was large, he found a little cabinet to sleep in since he had remembered the priest's advice. In the night, he heard sounds of fighting, and in the morning, the goblin-rat was dead in the middle of the temple, and all the cats he had painted had mouths wet and red from the blood.

When the priests found out, he was hailed as a hero, and he went on to become a famous artist; one who only painted cats!
Source (edited): "http://en.wikipedia.org/wiki/The_Boy_Who_Drew_Cats"

The Cat's Elopement

The Cat's Elopement is a Japanese fairy tale collected by David Brauns in *Japanische Marchen und Sagen*. Andrew Lang included it in *The Pink Fairy Book*.

Synopsis

A handsome cat named Gon, belonging to a music teacher, and a lovely cat named Koma, belonging to a lady, met and fell in love. Neither of their owners would sell one of them to the other owner, and they finally decided to elope. In the evening, they were threatened by a dog; Koma fled up a tree, while Gon stood his ground to protect her; a servant came by and carried off Gon to his mistress, the princess.

A snake had fallen in love with this princess, and annoyed her with its visits. One day, when it came to annoy her once again, Gon pounced on it and killed it. After, he saw a large cat harassing a smaller one. He went to rescue the small cat and found it was Koma. He brought her to the princess and told her their story. She wept with sympathy and kept them with her; when she married a prince, she told him their story, and the prince agreed to keep them always, so they lived happily, with their many kittens playing with the prince and princess's many children.
Source (edited): "http://en.wikipedia.org/wiki/The_Cat%27s_Elopement"

The Crab and the Monkey

The Crab and the Monkey, also known as **Monkey-Crab Battle** (さるかに合戦 *saru kani gassen*) or **The Quarrel of the Monkey and the Crab**, is a Japanese fairy tale. In the story, a sly monkey kills a crab, and is later killed in revenge by the crab's offspring. Retributive justice is the main theme of the story.

The Crab and the Monkey is included in the collection *Japanische Mahrchen*. Yei Theodora Ozaki included it in *Japanese Fairy Tales*, and Andrew Lang included a somewhat bowdlerized version in *The Crimson Fairy Book*.

Synopsis

While out walking, a crab finds a rice ball. A sly monkey persuades the crab to trade the rice ball for a persimmon seed. The crab is at first upset, but when she plants and tends the seed a tree grows that supplies abundant fruit. The monkey agrees to climb the tree to pick the fruit for the crab, but gorges himself on the fruit rather than sharing it with the crab. When the crab protests, the monkey hurls hard, unripe fruit at her. The shock of being attacked causes the crab to give birth just before she dies.

The crab's children seek revenge on the monkey. With the help of several allies — a chestnut, a millstone, a bee, and a cow pie — they go to the monkey's house. The chestnut hides himself on the monkey's hearth, the bee in the water pail, the cow pie on the dirt floor, and the millstone on the roof. When the monkey returns home he tries to warm himself on the hearth, but the chestnut strikes the monkey so that he burns himself. When the monkey tries to cool his burns at the water bucket, the bee stings him. When the startled monkey tries to run out of the house, the cow pie moves and trips him and the millstone falls from the roof, killing the monkey.

Variants

The name of the story, the list of allies, and the details of the attacks vary in different parts of Japan. For example, in Kansai one of the allies is a quantity of oil. In a version of the story published in a Japanese textbook in 1887, an egg appears in place of the chestnut and a piece of kelp replaces the cowpie. The egg attacks the monkey by exploding; the kelp slips from under his foot.

In the version of the story published by Andrew Lang, the crab gathers the unripe fruit and is not killed, but the monkey leaves her for dead.

Modern versions of the story often tone down the violence. The title "The Crab and the Monkey" or "The Story of the Monkey and the Crab" similarly reduce the violence apparent in the older "Monkey-Crab Battle" name.

Twentieth century Japanese novelist Ryunosuke Akutagawa wrote a short story based on the folktale in which, after avenging their mother's death by attacking the monkey, the crab children are arrested and face the death penalty.

In a completely different version of the story, when the monkey climbs the tree and takes all the persimmons the crab advises him to hang his basket of fruit from a branch. When the monkey hangs his basket on a thin branch, the branch breaks and the basket of fruit falls. The crab quickly carries the fruit off and crawls down a hole. The monkey decides to defecate on the crab, and sticks his buttocks down the hole. The crab quickly shaves the monkey's bottom, which is why to this day monkeys have hairless bottoms and hair grows on crabs' claws.

Similar stories involving a crab and a monkey, or a monkey and a toad, or other creatures seeking vengeance are found in China, Korea, and Mongolia, and among the Ainu.

Source (edited): "http://en.wikipedia.org/wiki/The_Crab_and_the_Monkey"

The Fountain of Youth (fairy tale)

LONG, LONG ago there lived somewhere among the mountains of Japan a poor woodcutter and his wife. They were very old, and had no children. Every day the husband went, alone to the forest to cut wood, while the wife sat weaving at home.

One day the old man went further into the forest than was his custom, to seek a certain kind of wood; and he suddenly found himself at the edge of a little spring he had never seen before. The water was strangely clear and cold, and he was thirsty; for the day was hot, and he had been working hard. So he doffed his huge straw-hat, knelt down, and took a long drink.

That water seemed to refresh him in a most extraordinary way. Then he caught sight of his own face in the spring, and started back. It was certainly his own face, but not at all as he was accustomed' to see it in the bronze mirror at home. It was the face of a very young man! He could not believe his eyes. He put up both hands to his head which had been quite bald only a moment before, when he had wiped it with the little blue towel he always carried with him. But now it was covered with thick black hair. And his face had become smooth as a boy's: every wrinkle was gone. At the same moment he discovered himself full of new strength. He stared in astonishment at the limbs that had been so long withered by age: they were now shapely and hard with dense young muscle. Unknowingly he had drunk of the Fountain of Youth; and that draught had transformed him.

First he leaped high and shouted for joy;-then he ran home faster than he had ever run before in his life. When he entered his house his wife was frightened;-because she took him for a stranger; and when he told her the wonder, she could not at once believe him. But after a long time he was able to convince her that the young man she now saw before her was really her husband; and he told her where the spring was, and asked her to go there with him.

Then she said:-"You have become so handsome and so young that you cannot continue to love an old woman;-so I must drink some of that water immediately. But it will never do for both of us to be away from the house at the same time. Do you wait here, while I go." And she ran to the woods all by herself.

She found the spring and knelt down, and began to drink. Oh! how cool and sweet that water was! She drank and drank and drank, and stopped for breath only to begin again.

Her husband waited for her impatiently;-he expected to see her come back changed into a pretty slender girl. But she did not come back at all. He got anxious, shut up the house, and went to look for her.

When he reached the spring, he could not see her. He was just on the point of returning when he heard a little wail in the high grass near the spring. He searched there and discovered his wife's clothes and a baby,-a very small baby, perhaps six months old.

For the old woman had drunk too deeply of the magical water; she had drunk herself far back beyond the time of youth into the period of speechless infancy.

He took up the child in his arms. It looked at him in a sad wondering way. He carried it home,-murmuring to it,-thinking strange melancholy thoughts.

Source (edited): "http://en.wikipedia.org/wiki/The_Fountain_of_Youth_(fairy_tale)"

The Husband of the Rat's Daughter

The Husband of the Rat's Daughter is a Japanese fairy tale. Andrew Lang included it in *The Brown Fairy Book*. It is Aarne-Thompson type 2031C, a chain tale or cumulative tale. Another story of this type is *The Mouse Turned into a Maid*.

Synopsis

Two rats had a remarkably beautiful daughter. In some variants, the father would have been happy to marry her to a rat of finer family, but the mother did not want her daughter to marry a mere rat; in others, they both agreed that she must marry the greatest being in the world. They offered her to the sun, telling him they wanted a son-in-law who was greater than all. The sun told them that he could not take advantage of their ignorance: the cloud, which blotted out his face, was greater. So they asked the cloud instead. The cloud told them that the wind freely blew it about. They asked the wind. The wind told them that the wall could easily stop it.

They asked the wall. The wall told them that a rat could reduce it to powder with its teeth. So they married her to a rat.
Source (edited): "http://en.wikipedia.org/wiki/The_Husband_of_the_Rat%27s_Daughter"

The Stonecutter

The Stonecutter is a Japanese folklore of unknown authorship. It is closely related to the themes of *The Fisherman and His Wife*, a well known fairy tale collected by the Brothers Grimm.

Origins

The exact author of *The Stonecutter* is unknown but the tale was already widespread in China and Japan before it was first translated by David Brauns in *Japanische Märchen und Sagen* (1885). Andrew Lang drew upon this source to publish his translation of the tale in *The Crimson Fairy Book* (1903). Variants appear across cultures and continents, including *The Fisherman and His Wife* by the Brothers Grimm.

According to the Aarne-Thompson classification system of fairy tales, *The Stonecutter* is a tale of type 555, *The Fisherman and His Wife*.

The story of the Stonecutter is a prime example of cyclical thinking in Eastern philosophy. While the similar cumulative tale *The Fisherman and His Wife* is explicitly moralist in tone, *The Stonecutter*'s lesson proceeds from a more philosophical viewpoint. At the end, the stonecutter simply realises that his greedy longings are futile because power is relative (compare: food chain).

The fisherman's wife however has no end to her ambition, and keeps asking for more influence; first nobleman, then king, then emperor, then pope until at last she wants to become God himself. The magic fish then punishes her (blasphemous) greed by sending her back to her poor hut (compare "hubris" in Greek mythology.)

*The Stonecutter'*s central theme is reflected in the popular hand game paper, rock, scissors, which (unsurprisingly) also has its origins in East Asia.
Source (edited): "http://en.wikipedia.org/wiki/The_Stonecutter"

The Tale of the Bamboo Cutter

The Tale of the Bamboo Cutter (竹取物語 *Taketori Monogatari*), also known as *Princess Kaguya* (かぐや姫 *Kaguya Hime*, 赫映姫), is a 10th century Japanese folktale. It is considered the oldest extant Japanese narrative and an early example of proto-science fiction.

It primarily details the life of a mysterious girl called Kaguya-hime, who was discovered as a baby inside the stalk of a glowing bamboo plant. She is said to be from Tsuki-no-Miyako (月の都 "The Capital of the Moon") and has unusual hair that shines like the moon.

Narrative

Taketori no Okina takes Kaguya-hime to his home, Drawn by Tosa Hiromichi, c. 1600

One day, while walking in the bamboo forest, an old, childless bamboo cutter called Taketori no Okina (竹取翁, "the Old Man who Harvests Bamboo") came across a mysterious, shining stalk of bamboo. After cutting it open, he found inside it a baby the size of his thumb. He rejoiced to find such a beautiful girl and took her home. He and his wife raised her as their own child and named her Kaguya-hime (かぐや姫 "radiant-night princess"). Thereafter, Taketori no Okina found that whenever he cut down a stalk of bamboo, inside he found a small nugget of gold. Soon he became rich, and Kaguya-hime grew from a small baby into a woman of ordinary size and extraordinary beauty. At first, Taketori no Okina tried to keep her away from outsiders, but over time the news of her beauty had spread.

Eventually, five princes came to Taketori no Okina's residence to ask for Kaguya-hime's hand in marriage. The princes eventually persuaded Taketori no Okina to tell a reluctant Kaguya-hime to choose one from among them. To this end, Kaguya-hime concocted impossible tasks for the princes to accomplish. She would agree to marry the prince who managed to bring her a specified item.

That night, Taketori no Okina told the five princes what each of them must bring. The first was told to bring her the stone begging bowl of the Buddha from India. The second was told to retrieve a jewelled branch from the island of Hōrai. The third was told to seek the legendary robe of the fire-rat of China. The fourth must retrieve a colored jewel from a dragon's neck. The final prince was told to find the cowrie which was born from swallows.

Realizing that it was an impossible task, the first prince returned with an expensive bowl, but after noticing that the bowl did not glow with holy light, Kaguya-hime saw through his deception. Likewise, two other princes attempted to deceive her with fakes, but also failed. The fourth gave up after encountering a storm, while the final prince lost his life in his attempt to retrieve the object.

After this, the Emperor of Japan, Mikado, came to see the strangely beautiful Kaguya-hime and, upon falling in love, asked her to marry him. Although he was not subjected to the impossible trials that thwarted the princes, Kaguya-hime rejected his request for marriage as well, telling him that she was not of his country and thus could not go to the palace with him. She stayed in contact with the Emperor, but continued to rebuff his requests.

That summer, whenever Kaguya-hime saw the full moon, her eyes filled with tears. Though her adoptive parents worried greatly and questioned her, she was unable to tell them what was wrong. Her behaviour became increasingly erratic until she revealed that she was not of this world and must return to her people on the Moon. In some versions of this tale, it is said that she was sent to the Earth as a temporary punishment for some crime, while others say it is because she was sent to earth for safety during a celestial war.

Kaguya-hime goes back to the Moon

As the day of her return approached, the Emperor set many guards around her house to protect her from the Moon people, but when an embassy of "Heavenly Beings" arrived at the door of Taketori no Okina's house, the many guards were blinded by a strange light. Kaguya-hime announced that, though she loves her many friends on Earth, she must return with the Moon people to her true home. She wrote sad notes of apology to her parents and to the Emperor, then gave her parents her own robe as a memento. She then took a small taste of the elixir of life, attached it to her letter to the Emperor, and gave it to a guard officer. As she handed it to him, the feather robe was placed on her shoulders, and all of her sadness and compassion for the people of the Earth were forgotten. The heavenly entourage took Kaguya-hime back to *Tsuki-no-Miyako* ("the Capital of the Moon") leaving her earthly foster parents in tears.

The parents became very sad and were soon put to bed sick. The guard officer returned to the Emperor with the items Kaguya-hime had given him as her last mortal act, and reported what had happened. The Emperor read her letter and was overcome with sadness. He asked his servants: "Which mountain is the closest place to Heaven?", to which one replied that the Great Mountain of Suruga Province is the closest place to Heaven. The Emperor ordered his men to take the letter to the summit of the mountain and burn it, with the hope that his message would reach the distant princess. The men were also commanded to burn the elixir of immortality since the Emperor did not desire to live forever without being able to see her. The legend has it that the word *immortality* (不死 *fushi*, or *fuji*) became the name of the mountain, Mount Fuji. It is also said that the kanji for the mountain, 富士山 (literally "Mountain Abounding with Warriors"), is derived from the Emperor's army ascending the slopes of the mountain to carry out his order. It is said that the smoke from the burning still rises to this day. (In the past, Mount Fuji was much more volcanically active than today.)

Literary connections

Elements of the tale were drawn from earlier stories. The protagonist Taketori no Okina, given by name, appears in the earlier poetry collection *Man'yōshū* (c. 759; poem# 3791). In it, he meets a group of women to whom he recites a poem. This indicates that there previously existed an image or tale revolving around a bamboo cutter and celestial or mystical women.

A similar retelling of the tale appears in the c. 12th century Konjaku Monogatarishū (volume 31, chapter 33), although their relation is under debate.

There have been suggestions that *The Tale of the Bamboo Cutter* is related to the tale of *Swan Lake*. This probably is due to Kaguya-hime wearing the *hagoromo* (羽衣 "feather robe") when she ascends to her homeland. But the hagoromo figures more famously in a group of tales known as the *hagoromo densetsu* (in one example recorded in the *Ōmi-no-kuni Fudoki* tells of a man who instructs his dog to steal the hagoromo of eight heavenly maidens while they were bathing, forcing one of them to become his bride). And the latter is remarkably similar to the tale of how Völundr the Smith and his brothers wedded the swan-maidens.

Banzhu Guniang

In 1957, *Jinyu Fenghuang* (金玉凤凰), a Chinese book of Tibetan tales, was published. In early 1970s, Japanese literary researchers became aware that "Banzhu Guniang" (班竹姑娘), one of the tales in the book, had certain similarities with *The Tale of the Bamboo Cutter*. Initially, many researchers thought that "Banzhu Guniang" must be related to *Tale of Bamboo Cutter*, although some were skeptical.

In 1980s, studies showed that the relationship is not as simple as initially thought. Okutsu provides extensive review of the research, and notes that the book *Jinyu Fenghuang* was intended to be for children, and as such, the editor took some liberties in adapting the tales. No other compilation of Tibetan tales contains the story.

A Tibet-born person wrote that he did not know the story. A researcher went to Sichuan and found that, apart from those who had already read "Jinyu Fenghuang", local researchers in Chengdu did not know the story. Tibetan informants in Aba did not know the story either.

Adaptations

Kon Ichikawa made a film of the story in 1987. Composer Robert Moran saw it and composed an opera based on it, *From the Towers of the Moon*.

Big Bird in Japan includes schoolchildren performing the play within the story.

The Hello Kitty television series has a simplified episode version of this story.

Source (edited): "http://en.wikipedia.org/wiki/The_Tale_of_the_Bamboo_Cutter"

Urashima Tarō

Portrait of Urashima Tarō by Utagawa Kuniyoshi

Urashima Tarō (浦島 太郎) is a Japanese legend about a fisherman who rescues a turtle and is rewarded for this with a visit to *Ryūgū-jō*, the palace of Ryūjin, the Dragon God, under the sea. He stays there for three days and, upon his return to his village, finds himself 300 years in the future.

History

The name *Urashima Taro* first appears in the 15th century (the Muromachi period), in the book *Otogizōshi*, but the story is much older, dating back to the 8th century (the Nara Period). These older books, such as *Nihon Shoki*, *Man'yōshū* and *Tango no Kuni Fudoki* (丹後国風土記) refer to Urashima Taro as *Urashimako*, though the story is the same. This represents a change in Japanese naming customs; in the previous eras, -ko (child) was used for both male and female names, while in later times it was mostly a female name element, replaced with -tarou (great youth) in boys' names.

Story

One day a young fisherman named Urashima Tarō is fishing when he notices a group of children torturing a small turtle. Tarō saves it and lets it to go back to the sea. The next day, a huge turtle approaches him and tells him that the small turtle he had saved is the daughter of the Emperor of the Sea, Ryūjin, who wants to see him to thank him. The turtle magically gives Tarō gills and brings him to the bottom of the sea, to the Palace of the Dragon God (Ryūgū-jō). There he meets the Emperor and the small turtle, who was now a lovely princess, Otohime.

Urashima Tarō illustration by Edmund Dulac

Tarō stays there with her for a few days, but soon wants to go back to his village and see his aging mother, so he asks Otohime permission to leave. The princess says she is sorry to see him go, but wishes him well and gives him a mysterious box called *tamatebako* which she tells him never to open. Tarō grabs the box, jumps on the back of the same turtle that had brought him there, and soon is at the seashore.

When he goes home, everything has changed. His home is gone, his mother has vanished, and the people he knew are nowhere to be seen. He asks if anybody knows a man called Urashima Tarō. They answer that they had heard someone of that name had vanished at sea long ago. He discovers that 300 years have passed since the day he left for the bottom of the sea. Struck by grief, he absent-mindedly opens the box the princess had given him, from which bursts forth a cloud of white smoke. He is suddenly aged, his beard long and white, and his back bent. From the sea comes the sad, sweet voice of the princess: "I told you not to open that box. In it was your old age ..." This story bears a striking similarity to many other tales, including that of Oisín and the earlier Chinese legend of Ranka.

Variations

As always with folklore, there are many different versions of this extremely famous story. In one, for example, after he turned into an old man he took the body of a crane, in another he ate a magic pill that gave him the ability to breathe underwater. In another version, he is swept away by a storm before he can rescue the turtle. Also, there is a version in which he dies in the process of aging (his body turns into dust), as no one can live 300 years.

Commemoration

Statue of Urashima Tarō in Mitoyo, Kagawa

A shrine on the western coast of the Tango Peninsula in northern Kyoto Prefecture, named Urashima Jinja, contains an old document describing a man, Urashimako, who left his land in 478

A.D. and visited a land where people never die. He returned in 825 A.D. with a Tamatebako. Ten days later he opened the box, and a cloud of white smoke was released, turning Urashimako into an old man.

Later that year, after hearing the story, Emperor Junna ordered Ono no Takamura to build a shrine to commemorate Urashimako's strange voyage, and to house the Tamatebako and the spirit of Urashimako.

The story influenced various works of fiction and a number of films. Among them are manga and anime such as *Dragonball Z*, *Clannad*, *Detective Conan*, *YuYu Hakusho*, *Urusei Yatsura*, *Love Hina* (whose lead male character is called Urashima Keitaro, and with a girl named Otohime Mutsumi), *Doraemon*, *Kamen Rider Den-O* (the namesake of the Imagin Urataros, given by Naomi), *Cowboy Bebop*, *Ookami-san to Shichinin no Nakamatachi* (One of the men in the Otogi Bank is called Urashima Tarou, he becomes the lover (although not extremely faithful) of a girl named Otohime, who is always being bullied with the nickname 'Turtle') *Ghost Sweeper Mikami* and *RahXephon*. It is retold in and used as the basis for the short story "Another Story" by Ursula K. Le Guin, published in her story collection *A Fisherman of the Inland Sea*, named for the character of this story.

Urashima Tarō is often referenced in Hideo Kojima's adventure video game *Policenauts*, and much of the game's plot elements were also inspired by the tale. In Clover Studio's action-adventure video game *Okami*, Amaterasu chases away a group of children who are bullying a fisherman by the name of Urashima who claims that he was taken away to the Dragon Palace by "Orca". Urashima tells Amaterasu that she can find Orca at the dock when the sun first rises. Amaterasu meets Orca, and after she proves herself worthy of the journey to the Dragon Palace by finding a hidden whirlpool, Orca take her to the Dragon Palace where she meets the queen of the Dragonians, Otohime.

The oldest known animated adaptation Urashima Tarō of the tale premiered in 1918.

During the 1970s, VARIG, a Brazilian airline, used him in a series of commercials, with the turtle bringing him to Brazil. After a while, he enjoys his stay, but grows old and longs to return to his home in Japan, so a woman (presumably the princess) gives him a box with an airplane ticket home, which when he opens also becomes much younger.

In the manga series One Piece, Vander Decken IX wished to use the box to age Princess Shirahoshi so she would be of marriageable age. Additionally, within the arc the names Otohime and Ryūgū-jō are shared with a character and location, respectively.

Source (edited): "http://en.wikipedia.org/wiki/Urashima_Tar%C5%8D"

Janghwa Hongryeon jeon

Janghwa Hongreyon jeon is a Joseon-era Korean folktale.

Story

Introduction

Once upon a time, there was a man named Bae whose wife had a dream where an angel gave her a beautiful flower. Nine months later, she gave birth to a pretty baby girl, who the couple named, "Janghwa" ("Rose Flower"). Two years later, they had another pretty girl, and named her "Hongryeon" ("Red Lotus"). Unfortunately, the mother died when Hongryeon was 5 years old; and soon thereafter, the father remarried to continue his line. The new stepmother was both ugly and cruel. She hated her stepdaughters, but hid those feelings, only to reveal them once she had three sons in a row, which gave her a good deal of power, and she abused the girls in every possible way. But Janghwa and Hongryeon never told their father about any of it.

Conflict

When Janghwa came of age and became engaged, Bae told his second wife to help Janghwa plan a wedding ceremony. Stepmother became angry, not wanting to spend a penny of "her family's money" or "her sons' future fortune" on Janghwa. So she came up with a dirty plan: One night when Janghwa was sleeping, Stepmother had her eldest son put a skinned dead rat in Janghwa's bed. Very early the next morning she brought Father to Janghwa's room, telling him she'd had a bad dream about her elder stepdaughter. When she pulled back the covers on Janghwa's bed, something that looked like a very bloody miscarriage shocked everybody in the room! Stepmother accused Janghwa of unchaste behavior, having an out-of-wedlock child by an unknown father. The father believed it. Janghwa did not know what to do, so she ran out of the room, out of the house, ran to a small pond in the nearby woods. Stepmother ordered her eldest son to follow Janghwa and push her into the pond. As Janghwa drowned, suddenly there came a huge tiger who attacked Stepmother's eldest son, taking one leg and one arm from him.

Stepmother had got what she wanted, Janghwa's death, but at the cost of her own son's health. She turned her anger upon Hongryeon, hating and abusing this remaining stepdaughter more than ever. Unable to bear this treatment on top of the loss of her beloved sister, Hongryeon soon followed Janghwa; her body was soon found in the same pond in which Janghwa had drowned.

After that, whenever a new mayor came to the village, he was found dead a day after his arrival. As this kept happening, mysterious rumors spread through the village, but no one knew for sure what had happened to the men or for what reason.

Resolution

A brave young man came to the village as a new mayor. He was aware of the deaths of predecessors, but he was not afraid for his own life. When night came, he was sitting in his room when his candle was suddenly blown out and gruesome noises filled the air. The door opened to reveal no one, at first, but then the new mayor saw 2 young female ghosts. He asked them who they were and why they had killed the previous mayors. Weeping, the elder sister explained that all they wanted was to let people know the truth: the elder girl had not been an unchaste girl who committed suicide in shame. She had been framed by her stepmother and murdered by her eldest half-brother. The mayor asked the ghost of Janghwa for any evidence of this. Janghwa told him to examine the miscarried fetus which Stepmother had shown to the villagers.

Conclusion

The next morning, the new mayor did what the sisters' ghosts had asked him to do. He summoned Father, Stepmother, and the eldest son and examined the fetus which Stepmother insisted had come from Janghwa's body. When he split it with a knife, it was revealed to be a rat. Stepmother and her eldest son were sentenced to death. Father, however, was set free because the mayor thought Father had known nothing of Stepmother's evil plan and in fact was just another victim.

Years later, Father married again. On the night of his third wedding, he saw his two daughters in a dream. They said that since things were as they should be, they wanted to come back to him. Nine months later, Father's third wife delivered twin girls. Father named these twins "Janghwa" and "Hongryeon" and loved them very much. The new family lived happily ever after.

Films

The story has been adapted to film a number of times, and formed the basis of the 2003 Kim Ji-woon film *A Tale of Two Sisters* and the 2009 American remake, "The Uninvited".

- *Jang-hwa and Hong-ryeon* (1924)
- *Story of Jang-hwa and Hong-ryeon* (1936)
- *Janghwa Heungryeonjeon* (1956)
- *Dae Jang-hwa Hong-ryeon jeon* (1962)
- *Janghwa Hongryeonjeon* (1972)
- *A Tale of Two Sisters* (2003)
- *The Uninvited* (2009)

Source (edited): "http://en.wikipedia.org/wiki/Janghwa_Hongryeon_jeon"

The Fox Sister

The Fox Sister is a Korean fairy tale.

Synopsis

A man had three sons and no daughter. He prayed for a daughter, even if she were a fox. His wife gave birth to a daughter, but when the girl was six, one of their cows died every night. He set his oldest son to watch. The boy watched, and told him that his sister did it, by pulling the liver out of the cow and eating it. His father accused him of having fallen asleep and having a nightmare. He threw out his son. The second son was set to watch, and nothing happened until the moon was full again, but then the sister struck, and the second son ended the same. The youngest son was set and claimed that their sister had gone to the outhouse, and the cow must have died from seeing the moon.

The older brothers wandered until they met a Buddhist monk, who sent them back with three magical bottles. They found the sister living alone; she told them their parents and brother had died, and implored them to stay. Finally, she persuaded them to stay the night and somehow made a rich meal for them. In the night, the older brother was woken by the sounds of chewing. He rolled over, saw the meal, and realized that they had been eating corpses. The sister stood over his dead brother, eating his liver. She told him that she needed only one more to become a human. He fled. He threw the white bottle behind him, and it became a thicket of thorns. As a fox, she made her way through it. He threw the blue bottle behind him, and trapped her in a river, but as a fox, she swam ashore. He threw the red bottle behind, and she was trapped in fire. It burned her until she was no more than a mosquito.

Commentary

In the Confucian view, it may be interpreted on the importance of keeping daughters in their lowly place and favoring the more important sons over them.

Source (edited): "http://en.wikipedia.org/wiki/The_Fox_Sister"

Preeta Samarasan

Preeta Samarasan Malaysian author writing in English whose first novel, *Evening Is the Whole Day*, won the Hopwood Novel Award (while she was doing her MFA at the University of Michigan), was a finalist for the Commonwealth Writers Prize 2009, and was on the longlist for the Orange Prize for Fiction.. A number of short stories have also appeared in different magazines; "Our House Stands in a City of Flowers" won the Asian American Writer's Workshop/Hyphen (magazine) short-story award in 2007.

Life

Samarasan was born in Batu Gajah. Her father was a schoolteacher in Ipoh in Malaysia, where she attended the SM (Sekolah Menengah) Convent School. In 1992, she won a United World College scholarship and went to the Armand Hammer United World College of the American West in New Mexico, USA. After graduating in 1994, she went to Hamilton College, and then joined the Ph.D. program in musicology at the Eastman School of Music, University of Rochester. She was working on Gypsy music festivals in France, for which she was awarded a Council for European Studies fellowship in 2002. Meanwhile, in 1999 she had started work on her novel, and eventually she gave up on her dissertation to write. In 2006 she graduated from the MFA program in creative writing from the University of Michigan, where she worked on polishing her novel.

Evening Is the Whole Day

Evening Is the Whole Day focuses on the dark secrets of an affluent Malaysian Indian family (also living in Ipoh), and has been praised for its lyrical, inventive language, often using untranslated Tamil words, and using aspects of Bahasa syntax, such as reduplicatives as intensifiers. The "ambitious spiraling plot" has also come in for praise. Like servants in some other recent novels (Triton in Romesh Gunesekera's *Reef* and Ugwu in Chimamanda Ngozi Adichie's Half of a Yellow Sun), the servant girl Chellam emerges as an important character. The story also describes the May 13 race riots of 1969 using the cameo characters "Rumour" and "Fact". It was nominated for the Commonwealth Writers Prize in 2009 for the Best First Book Award.

Samarasan currently lives in the Limousin region of France with her husband and daughter

Source (edited): "http://en.wikipedia.org/wiki/Preeta_Samarasan"

Madschun

Madschun is a Turkish fairy tale from Andrew Lang's *The Olive Fairy Book*.

Once, there was a young man who, even from childhood, had never grown any hair. One day, he saw the Sultan's daughter and became determined to marry her. He first sent his mother to tell the Sultan that her son wanted to marry his daughter. The Sultan was intrigued by the request, and told the woman to send her son. However, by the time the son arrived, the Sultan's interest had waned, and he only wanted to be rid of the boy. So he told the boy that he must first gather all the birds of the world and bring them to the Sultan's garden, which had no birds. After wandering for a time, the boy met a dervish, and asked his help. The dervish told him to go to a huge cypress tree down the road, and hide in its shadow until he heard a huge rush of wings. This would be all the birds in the world coming for a rest. He was to wait until they were sitting, then say the word "madschun", which would cause them to freeze and become motionless. He could then gather the birds and take them to the palace. And that is what the boy did. The sultan was a little dismayed. He told the boy that he could marry the princess - after he grew a full head of hair. Upset, the boy went home and brooded until he heard that the princess was to marry the son of the wazir. At this, he sneaked into the palace, found where the princess, the wazir's son, and some others were waiting, and said "Madschun". This froze all of them to the spot. The Sultan sent for a magician to explain what had happened, and the magician told him that it was because the Sultan had mistreated the boy. The Sultan sent for the boy at once, and the boy, hiding nearby, raced home. The boy told his mother that she was to tell the sultan's messengers that the boy had left awhile ago, and that if they asked her to go look for the boy, she was to say that she was too poor to travel. She did this, and the messengers gave her a bag of gold for expenses and asked her help. After they left, the boy went to the palace, freed everyone, and married the princess.

Source (edited): "http://en.wikipedia.org/wiki/Madschun"

The Boy Who Found Fear At Last

The Boy Who Found Fear At Last is a Turkish fairy tale collected by Ignaz Kunos in *Türkische Volksmärchen*. Andrew Lang included it in *The Olive Fairy Book*

Synopsis

A woman had an only son. During a storm, she told him to shut the door because she felt frightened. He asked her what she meant. When she could not make him understand, he set out to find the fear she told him of.

He found robbers and sat with them by their fire. When they realized he did not fear them, they gave him the ingredients and sent him to a churchyard to cook him a cake. A hand from the grave asked for it, but the boy said that he did not give the food of the living to the dead, and rapped it with a spoon. Then they sent him to a pool. He found there a swing hanging over the pool with a child on it. A maiden told him that it was her brother and asked if she could climb on his shoulders to get him down; when he did, she started to strangle him with her feet. He threw her off, and she lost a bracelet that he took up.

He went on. An ogre demanded the bracelet, as it was his. They went before a judge, who decreed that neither of them had a right to it, and he would keep it until one of them brought him its partner. So the ogre and the boy both had to leave it.

He met up with a ship being wrecked. He swam to it and had the frightened sailors lower him into the sea. He found there a sea-maiden dragging down the ship. He freed the ship and chained her up.

He found a garden in which three doves flew in, and turned into maidens; one had been the hand in the graveyard, the second the one with the bracelet, and the third the seamaiden. They toasted his health. He appeared to them, and they gave him the matching bracelet.

He went on for a long time, but never found fear. One day he came to a crowded city. He was told the king had died and had no heir, so a pigeon would be released. Whoever it perched on would be king. It perched on the boy. He had a vision of himself trying to make his poor subjects rich, his bad ones good, and never succeeding and never be able to do as he wished. He was terrified, but they released more pigeons and they all flew to him.

Having found fear, the young man submitted to being king.

Source (edited): "http://en.wikipedia.org/wiki/The_Boy_Who_Found_Fear_At_Last"

The Silent Princess

The Silent Princess is a Turkish fairy tale. Andrew Lang included it in *The Olive Fairy Book*. It contains inset tales that are similar to ones in Arabian Nights.

Synopsis

A pasha's son one day was playing with his golden ball, and three times broke a woman's pitcher. She cursed him to fall in love with the silent princess, and vanished. As he grew older, he wondered who the silent princess was, and in time wondered so much that he became ill. His father asked what had made him ill, in hopes that it would reveal his cure, and the son revealed the curse and asked permission to search the world for her. His father granted it.

The prince set out with an old steward, and after three old men gave them directions and warnings, he finally found the mountain where the princess sat behind seven veils and never spoke. The mountain was surrounded by human bones and mourners, who warned the prince that he needed the leave of the sultan to be escorted into the princess's presence, and the bones could tell him the effect of his decision. The prince could not think of a way to make her talk, so he put off speaking to the sultan until he had one.

While there, the prince bought a nightingale, and found it could talk. It asked him why he was so sad, and when he told the bird his story, she told him to go, and when the princess would not speak, he must tell her he would instead converse with the candlestick, where the nightingale would be hidden. The prince obeyed. The princess would not speak to him, so he spoke to the candlestick, and the nightingale said it had been years since anyone had spoken to her, so she would tell him a story.

She described how a king set three wooers to learn something in six months, and the cleverest would win the princess. One learned how to travel a year's journey in an hour; another to see things at a distance; the third to cure any illness. They met again, and the second saw the princess was dying, the first brought the third to her, and the third one cured her. Then the prince and the nightingale argued whether the second or the third had done the better, until the princess burst out that it would have been useless without the first, who should have her.

A slave ran to tell the sultan, but the princess persuaded him, by signs, to make the prince make her speak three times. She destroyed the candlestick.

The next night, the nightingale hid on a pillar, and the prince talked to it. The nightingale told of a woman who had scorned wooers for many years, until she found a white hair and decided to pick one. She set them to tasks. She told the first wooer that her father had died, and proved to be a wizard because his grave was empty; the man's task was to lay in the grave three hours, so the woman would be free of him. He lay down there at once. She told a second wooer that a wizard had taken the place of her father's body in the grave; if he stood over the wizard with a stone and smashed his head if he moved, she would be free. The man took such a stone and sat down at once. She told a third wooer that a wizard had taken the place of her father's body in the grave, but if he brought him before her, she would be free. He immediately brought the body before her. Then the nightingale argued whether the second or third wooer had done the best, until the princess said it was the first. That day, she destroyed the pillar.

The third night, the nightingale hid in the curtains by the door, and told the prince of a carpenter, a tailor, and a student who lived in the same house. The carpenter made a statue of a woman; the tailor dressed it; the student prayed to heaven that she might become a living woman. The nightingale and prince quarreled over whether the carpenter or the tailor had the best right to marry her, until the princess said that the student's prayer meant he should win her.

At that, her veils fell, and she agreed to marry the prince. They sent for the woman whose pitchers he had broken, and she became a nurse to their children.

Source (edited): "http://en.wikipedia.org/wiki/The_Silent_Princess"

The Hundred-knot Bamboo Tree

The Hundred-knot Bamboo Tree (also **The Bamboo of 100 Joints**) (Vietnamese: *Cây tre trăm đốt*) is a Vietnamese fable and parable, and part of Vietnamese oral tradition. The story is included in anthologies of Vietnamese stories.

Story

The story is about a laborer who is exploited by a wealthy landowner. In order to keep and motivate the laborer, the landowner promises to reward him with marriage to his daughter after three years of labor. When the time for marriage arrives, the landowner breaks his promise by offering his daughter to another man. When the laborer complains, the landowner tries to trick him again by sending him in search of a bamboo stalk with one hundred segments, again promising him his daughter if the laborer can find the bamboo stalk. After divine intervention, the laborer triumphs in the end.

Source (edited): "http://en.wikipedia.org/wiki/The_Hundred-knot_Bamboo_Tree"

The Story of Tam and Cam

The Story of Tấm and Cám (Vietnamese: *Tấm Cám*) is a Vietnamese fairy tale collected by L. T. Bach-Lan in *Vietnamese Legends*.

It is Aarne-Thompson type 510A. Others of this type include *Cinderella*, *Fair, Brown and Trembling*, *Finette Cendron*, *The Golden Slipper*, *The Green Knight*, *Katie Woodencloak*, *Rushen Coatie*, *The Sharp Grey Sheep*, and *The Wonderful Birch*.

Synopsis

Once upon a time there was a young girl named Tấm, whose mother died early and so her father remarried. Soon after, her stepmother gave birth to a daughter named Cám. When Tấm's father died, stepmother began to abuse Tấm and forced her to do all the housework, while Cám lived luxuriously. Stepmother's hatred of Tam was intensified by the fact that Tam was much more beautiful and fair than her own daughter Cám, even though Tấm was forced to do all the laboring under the sun.

One day, stepmother sent Tấm and Cám to fish, promising to reward the girl who caught the most fish with a new, red silk Áo yếm. Cám knew her mother would never punish her and so played carelessly while Tấm worked hard fishing. When Cám noticed all the fish Tấm had caught, Cám advised Tấm to wash the mud out of her hair or else she would be scolded by mother. As Tấm washed her hair, Cám poured all the fish Tấm had caught into her own basket and ran home.

Upon discovering she had been tricked, Tấm sobbed until the Goddess of Mercy (or in some versions, the Buddha) appeared to her and comforted her. She told Tấm to look into her basket to discover the one remaining little carp. She told Tam to take the carp home and put it into the well at the back of the house, reciting a special poem/greeting whenever she came to feed it.

Everyday, Tấm would come out to the well a few times to feed the carp, always reciting the greeting beforehand so that the carp would come up from the water. The carp grew fatter everyday that Tấm fed it, and stepmother began to suspect Tấm's behavior. One day, stepmother sneaked out close to where Tấm was feeding the fish. She waited until Tấm was gone, and went over to the well, finding nothing. Stepmother repeated the greeting she had heard Tam reciting and to her delight, saw the carp come up from the water. Stepmother caught and killed it to put in her rice porridge.

When Tấm discovered this, she broke into sobs. The Goddess of Mercy again appeared to Tấm and consoled her, and instructed her to salvage the bones of the carp and bury them in four separate jars underneath each corner of her bed.

A short while later, the king hosted a large celebration. Tấm pleaded to go along with Cám and stepmother, but stepmother schemed to keep Tấm at home. Stepmother mixed together countless black and green beans (in other versions husked and white rice) and ordered Tấm to sort them out before she was allowed to go (adding that Tấm did not have any decent clothes to attend the event anyway). Tấm waited until Cám and stepmother had gone for a while and called out to the Goddess of Mercy, who appeared and turned the nearby flies into sparrows that sorted the beans for Tấm. Tấm was then told to dig up the four jars from the corners of her bed, and found extravagant treasures in each, including a beautiful silk dress, jewelry, golden slippers and even a horse! Tấm dressed herself splendidly and made her way to the celebration, but in her excitement she dropped a single slipper into the river.

The slipper flowed along the river until it was picked up by one of the king's attendants. The king marveled at the beautiful slipper and proclaimed that any maiden at the celebration whose foot fit the slipper would be made into his first wife. Every eligible lady at the celebration tried on the slipper, including Cám, but all to no avail. Suddenly, a beautiful young girl dressed in a magnificent silk gown appeared whose foot fit perfectly into the slipper (not to mention on her other foot was adorned the corresponding slipper of the same make). Stepmother and Cám were shocked to discover the mysterious lady was no other than Tấm! Tấm was immediately brought on the royal palanquin into the imperial palace for a grand wedding celebration, right in front of her seething stepmother and stepsister.

On Tấm's father's death anniversary, Tấm proved her filial duty and made a short visit home to honor the anniversary with her family, despite the abuse she had suffered at the hands of stepmother. Stepmother asked Tấm to climb an areca tree and gather its betel nuts for her late father's altar. Tấm obeyed and as she climbed to the top of the tree, stepmother took an axe and chopped the tree down, so that Tấm fell to her death. By tradition, Cám was married into the palace in place of her late sister. Tấm had reincarnated into a nightingale and followed her sister into the palace.

The king remained despondent and dearly missed his late wife, while Cám tried hard to please him. One day, a palace maid hung out the king's dragon robe to the sun, when the nightingale appeared to sing a song to remind the maid to be careful with her husband's gown. The bird's song captivated everyone who listened to it, and even drew the attention of the king. The king called out to the nightingale to land in the wide sleeves of his robe if it really was the spirit of his late wife. The nightingale did exactly as the king had asked and ever since then, it was put into a golden cage where the king spent most of his days as it sang songs to him. Cám became increasingly incensed and asked her mother what she should do. Her mother instructed her to catch the bird and feed it to a cat. Cám did as she was told and after skinning it, threw the feathers over the gate of the palace.

From the feathers rose a beautiful white cedar tree. Its shade was so soothing that the King ordered a hammock to be made under it, and to his immense liking, he always dreamed about his late wife Tấm when he rested under that tree. Cám was jealous again when she learned about it so she told her mother, whom instructed Cám to chop down the tree and make a loom out of its wood. But later on when Cám sat on the loom and tried to weave some cloth, the decorative crow on the loom spoke with Tấm's voice, accusing Cám of stealing her husband.

Following her mother's advice, Cám burned the loom and buried its ash far outside the palace. From where the ashed was buried, a persimmon tree rose, bearing only a single but magnificent fruit. A poor old woman who worked as a water vendor walked by one day and saw it, begging it to fall to her, and promising that she would not to eat it, only admire it. Indeed it fell to her, and she did not eat it. The next day, the old woman found that when she came home from her errands, the housework was done while she was gone and there was a hot meal waiting for her. This miracle happened continuously for a month, so one day, the old lady pretended to leave but stayed back to spy, when she saw Tấm emerge from the fruit and begin to do the household chores. The old woman emerged and tore up the peel so Tấm could no longer turn back.

One day, the king, lost while hunting, stopped by the hut. The old woman offered him betel, and when the king saw how the betel had been prepared, in the peculiar special way his late queen had always prepared it; he inquired as to whom had prepared the betel. The old woman told him her daughter had done it, and the king made her produce the daughter, and saw it was Tấm. He was overjoyed and Tấm was brought back into the palace as the king's first wife.

Cám was distressed and saw that Tam was as beautiful and pale as ever. She begged Tấm to reveal her secret of how she was so beautiful and fair-skinned, and that she would do anything to be as fair. Tấm told her it was simple and that she would just have to jump into a basin of boiling water. Cám did and died a horrible death.

Alternate ending

In some versions of the story, there is an extended ending where Tấm also exacts revenge on her stepmother. After Cám is boiled alive, her body is pounded and prepared as part of a pungent Vietnamese fermented sauce known as mắm; usually it is made from fish. Tấm sends a jar of this dish to her stepmother, claiming it to be a "gift from Cám." Every day, the stepmother ate some of the delicious sauce with her food.

One day, a crow flew by the Stepmother's house and rested on her roof. It cried out: "Delicious! The mother is eating her own daughter's flesh Is there any left? Give me some."

The stepmother was enraged, but when she finally reached the bottom of the jar, she discovered Cám's skull inside and immediately died of shock.

Source (edited): "http://en.wikipedia.org/wiki/The_Story_of_Tam_and_Cam"